Publication Number 1 in the "On Targe **Series of Sports Publications**

GW00646749

On Target for

UNDERSTANDING WINNING ARCHERY

Al Henderson

Edited by Glenn Helgeland

Library of Congress Catalog Card Number: 82-074190

ISBN: 0-913305-00-6

TARGET COMMUNICATIONS CORPORATION
7626 W. Donges Bay Rd.
Mequon, Wisconsin 53092

Copyright © 1983 by Target Communications Corporation
All rights reserved.

No part of this book may be reproduced in any form
or by any means, except for the inclusion of brief
quotations in a review, without permission in writing
from the publisher. Printed in the United States of
America by Ripon Community Printers, Ripon,
Wisconsin.

Portions of this book are reprinted from *Archery
World* magazine, with their permission.

Photographs by Glenn Helgeland
Art by Scott Samson and Judy Helgeland

i

Publisher's Note:

It was my pleasure, in 1972 as *Archery World* (now *Bowhunting World*) magazine's editor, to introduce Al Henderson (as a new member of the technical staff) and his coaching philosophy to thousands of reader-archers who had not previously been fortunate enough to have heard him talk about his favorite sport. What he had to say about shooting archery was worth reading and heeding.

In 1976, we began his regular coaching column which enabled him to go into more detail on his philosophy.

Now, Target Communications publishes Al's book, UNDERSTANDING WIN-NING ARCHERY. In this book, he challenges you to think and try, just as he challenges his students.

"Some of my comments may appear unorthodox at first - but the techniques and philosophy have worked with a wide enough variety of people and personalities that I am confident of what I believe and say here," he says.

"We often let ourselves fall into a mental rut, but the last thing a shooter or coach needs to do is get into that kind of rut. An open, understanding mind is essential for success."

I hope you enjoy reading this book as much as I have enjoyed editing and publishing it.

Glenn Helgeland, President
Target Communications Corporation
Mequon, Wisconsin

Dedication

To all the sages and students from whom I have learned all that is in the pages of this book.

To the two men who badgered, cajoled, insisted and pushed me to write this book —

> Glenn Helgeland for his understanding of what my mental approach and shooting message to you is, and the work needed to put it together.

> Dave Staples for his insistence through the years for me to share what I believe in.

These two guys are the reason this book exists.

And to my wife Violette, who always reinforced my burning desire to promote my favorite sport.

How to get the most personal benefit from this book.

There is a considerable amount of information in this book to mull over, think about, try out. Because of that, don't rush it. Take a little bit and work on it, then come back for more when you're ready to advance another step.

Carry it in your tackle box. Read it. Digest it. Study it. Get involved with it. Use it as a reference book; check back in it to help evaluate your own progress. **Make** it pay dividends for you.

How you feel about your archery self and your shooting is the best judge of how well you're doing.

We want you to feel good. Read, think and enjoy.

My Coaching Philosophy

The procedures I use in training people are guided by a philosophy which has evolved over a period of years. The **basic principle** is the same as it was when revealed to me many years ago: **"Think right, think all of the time and victory is yours."** That is a positive approach which works.

If you were to come to me today for help and ask me if I thought you would ever make a good shooter, I would have to ask **you** in turn what you thought, because that is the determining factor. I sincerely believe that **you can shoot with the best of them if . . .**

If you first have a real **desire** to learn to shoot well.

If you are willing to **work** for it. You can't only dream. Dreams are important, but you must do something about them.

If you are willing to adopt as your cry **"practice, practice, practice . . . but think, understand and practice right."**

If you will sincerely strive to **develop and maintain correct mental attitudes.** Correct mental attitudes will become habits and develop into realistic optimism, honest self-confidence and the ability to think through each shot.

When you can honestly answer these questions with a solid yes, you are on your way.

If you were literally a student of mine, I would have, during our initial interview, inquired about the specific area of your interest. You would have defined your expectations. I'd know just what you were shooting for — competition, the challenge, a social pastime, a hunting possibility, an easily available exercise.

My diagnosis of your particular needs would depend upon the information you give me and the knowledge I gain from watching you shoot.

You will have greater natural skill for some of the phases of this great sport than for others. It will be easier for you to perform certain of the mechanics necessary for good form than it will be to perform other mechanics. We would need to discover these strengths and weaknesses and allocate training sessions and practice accordingly.

In whichever branch of archery you prefer, I firmly believe that if you adhere to the positive **"think right, shoot right"** method of **approaching and solving all problems as they arise** you will do well. As an extremely valuable fringe benefit, you will have established general habits of self-confidence and optimism that will give you the power to cope with any life situation.

Al Henderson

Contents

CHAPTER FOUR: Turning Negatives To Positives

CHAPTER FIVE: Equipment, Form And Your Mind

CHAPTER SIX: Blazing A Tournament Trail

CHAPTER SEVEN: Coaches And Students

Chapter One: Building Blocks of Winning Archery

Your mental mastery

The mental part of archery is much greater than we often believe it is. The physical part is important, and the mechanical (equipment) part is important. However, the mental part controls what the physical does and thus also ultimately controls the mechanical part.

That's why it is so important to **understand** what you're doing, understand what the mind does. I would like to be a part of helping all archers understand that, ultimately, the mind does it. In learning to understand and shoot winning archery, you never can put too much emphasis on your mental aspect, your mental control.

You'll not get the best from yourself unless you **understand,** and you can't understand unless your mind is working and accepting what it should accept.

One of the keys to this is to honestly point the finger at our individual selves as a finger needs to be pointed. We can't be scared of that. We have to make a decision. We have to admit to ourselves the good and the not-so-good things we're doing in our shooting. We have to understand that, "Yes, I made that mistake, and I can correct it," or "Boy, I sure put that together right."

However, many shooters cannot bring themselves to do that. That's focusing a very bright light on their inner selves, and they're uncomfortable in that light. It **has** to be done.

Oddly, or maybe not so oddly, I've found that often the brightest people are the ones who don't want to admit their mind is doing this, that or the other thing to their overall performance. They can find too many reasons to avoid being honest with themselves; they cannot accept the truth.

Good equipment is important, but it does only what it is set up to do. No archer has ever shot as well as his or her archery tackle was capable of shooting. If I were forced to place a percentage estimate on equipment, I'd say it is only around 10 percent of the total picture of understanding winning archery. That does not, however, take any importance away from it. It is a cog in the entire wheel; it is complementary to your mental process.

● Linda Myers, left, prepares her next shot as Luann Ryon, right, who already has put the shot together, aims for another 10 on her away to the 1976 Women's Gold Medal in Olympic Archery, Montreal.

When you step up to that white line, you're not tired and you're not ill. Even when you think you're ill, you're not ill. When you step to that line, you have only one thing in mind — to make one right shot. Then, after that, to shoot another one.

If you come home from work or school, feeling exhausted, planning to get a good night's sleep, what happens when a good friend unexpectedly shows up? Maybe one you haven't seen for a while? Right . . . your batteries are charged instantly and you have a long, enjoyable night on the town. The next day, all you can talk about is the fun you had.

What changed? Only one thing — attitude. Your **mind** changed it.

And that's what I want to have understood by everyone reading this book . . . what your mind will do **for** you and what your mind will do **to** you. Your mind can do amazing things in your favor **if you will let it.**

Anyone who has ever shot competition will know that sometimes you'll make a mistake . . . your drawing hand was wrong, your bow hand, whatever . . . but the arrow goes squarely in the middle of the gold. How did you do that? You can do that two, three, four times maybe, but then you'll start thinking about it and it's all gone. We used to call that "tricking them in." When we had ourselves under control, letting our subconscious and trained mind and muscles do their thing, we had it working right. But the instant we tried to figure it out, instead of just trusting ourself enough to continue doing it without analysis, it was lost.

Building Blocks

When you get into this, you're dealing with different levels of the conscious and subconscious mind. The reason we lose the "tricking them in" touch is that we **consciously** don't understand how the **subconscious** did it. We can't simply accept it, so our mind first tries to deny it or figure out what happened. We get too technical and lose the naturalness. We just plain can't accept that our mind and our muscles, working together, can do those fantastic things. We have at our fingertips the ability to do anything we want — in archery and in life if we will allow ourselves to do so.

Challenge yourself

Setting challenges is an individual thing. A coach can give you, the shooter, a challenge if he or she knows how you're put together mentally. However, since everyone responds in individual ways, there is no wide guideline.

How do you challenge yourself? You do, don't you?

Some shooters fail to challenge themselves. I don't know why. Is it a matter of intestinal fortitude?

Or is it a matter of reaching a level you're content with, then staying at that level? If that is the case, then you know yourself well and will set yourself whatever challenges are necessary to remain at that level.

However, I seem to get the "I'd like to do better" response from everyone, even from those who just go out and shoot and horse around and have a good time and appear to be content with that.

So . . . know yourself . . . challenge yourself.

Your body will dictate your shooting form

There are a great many things that need to be taken into consideration when a coach is confronted with a new student.

All too often, I think a great many people start out the first lesson by trying to correct the most noticeable things that appear to be bad shooting form. Too many times there is a lot of frustrating work that goes on far too long without ever arriving at the **look** a coach thinks he should see in that form for that student. The reason for this waste of time is that he did not analyze the student from head to toe in minute detail before he ever made corrections in that person's present form.

What I am saying is that no two people are **exactly** alike. **Coaches** and **shooters** must realize this. Physical characteristics are similar but not the same. Somewhere in that physical makeup is a difference that may make it impossible for the coach to make the shooting form look like "the book" says it should look.

Failure to analyze a particular shooter — and let the form fit that individual regardless of what it looks like — keeps many potential champions down in the mediocre class.

If an effort is made to analyze each student separately, and if these differences are made to work to the advantage of the shooter, that shooter can get better scores with less effort.

Let's explore some of the differences in our anatomy and talk about the effects they might have on an archer's form.

The position of the head as it sits on the neck . . . the angle of the neck as it comes out of the body . . . the breastbone (sternum) may be flat or slightly barrelled . . . the size of the breasts . . . the size of the shoulders and upper arm, fat or muscular . . . the jawbone, square or round . . . the chin, narrow, jutting forward or receding . . . the neck, long or short.

These are only a few items which must be explored when putting an individual's form together. Exploring with the thought that you cannot change neck, chest or shape of the jawbone, you can sometimes by manipulation offset one with the other. This is rewarding to the student and will help you quickly recognize when there is no easy solution and you must "make do" with what you have.

If the jawbone is square (not narrow), the shooter has no trouble putting the hand under the jaw for a good solid anchor. If the jawbone and chin (the face) is narrow, then the shooter must bend the wrist of the drawing arm to get under the jawbone. A bent wrist is not conducive to a good, smooth, relaxed release. A ledge finger tab can in most cases fix this. There are exceptions. Side-of-face anchor could also be helpful in some cases.

If the neck is short, the shooter may have a lot of trouble anchoring in the center of the chin and nose and in turning his/her head to align the string. A ledge tab used with a side-of-face anchor, or some modification of it, will relieve the shooter from screwing his head around in a neck-twisting, uncomfortable position. Those who insist that the center of the chin and the nose must touch the string are not always helping the shooter who has a short neck. Short necks can also produce string interference on the body.

Shoulders and upper arms vary in size, and one that is overly fat or muscular may cause string interference at full draw. Generally, this is relieved if some degree of open stance is used.

The next three things tie together to make up a lot of different ways that, collectively or individually, can produce handicaps for the shooter. These combinations can be baffling sometimes in that two people may look about the same, but one has a problem and the other doesn't. Only by analyzing each other separately and then comparing the two can we see the difference in the problem and a solution for it.

4

The neck comes out of the body at different angles, from straight up to quite a bit forward. Line up a straight line between the point of the shoulders and see where the head is in relation to that line (with student standing naturally and at ease). If the natural position is like a soldier saluting, the line will run about through the student's ears. Not many are that straight up. Most are somewhere forward of that line, and that has a bearing upon where the head is. That will help or hinder the string clearance, length of draw, etc.

Heads are positioned upon necks at different angles. Some people naturally hold their head high. Some always appear to be looking down. This also controls, to some extent, string clearance and draw length. It could be that none of this will matter much. It will depend on the **remainder of the body** and what it does to help or hinder.

The breastbone (sternum) plays an important part in archery form because its shape has a lot to do with string clearance for a lot of people. If the breastbone protrudes forward to some degree, problems may become more evident depending on the size, shape, degree or angle of everything else involved.

The size of the female breasts is very important to good shooting form because of the interference of the breasts with the string at full draw. A flat chest with large breasts could cause trouble. A barrelled chest with small breasts may not, and the reverse may be true depending on the position of the head, neck, chin, etc. This sometimes can be greatly relieved if the problem is analyzed properly and steps taken to correct it. Those steps may not follow the book exactly, but they might make the person shoot better.

The thing that makes string interference so important is that there is no way to keep the string from making a loop to the left toward the shooter's body (right-hand shooter) as it comes off the fingertips on its way forward.

The size of this loop or movement is dictated by the size of the string, the size of the fingertips, draw weight of the bow, the speed at which the string is released and the degree of the relaxation in the release fingers.

No way can anyone loose the string fast enough to prevent this movement; however, a perfect "live" relaxed release would cause the least loop or movement. This movement goes toward the shooter first, picking up interference on whatever the shooter is wearing — be it loose fitting clothing, soft material or even flesh (if you want to prove this movement by wearing a halter top). Any interference is hard to control to maintain the consistency that is necessary for good shooting.

We must analyze to ascertain what can be done with what we have that will offset as much as possible those things which are negative to the effort. There is a combination of things in every shooter's form that, if found and used, will help him or her shoot better.

Building Blocks

It takes a lot of work. It is sometimes slow in showing up, but it is rewarding to both coach and student.

Just remember this: The **art** of analyzing can only be perfected by the experience of trial and error.

Every problem actually is an opportunity for improvement.

Matched and tuned equipment — important steps toward success

If you want to become a good shooter, or if you are a good shooter and want to become a better one, or if you aspire to reach that highest of goals — the Olympic Team, and a chance at those gold medals — you must understand the importance of **matching** and **tuning** your equipment. Each piece of equipment must be matched, one with the other, and the whole of it matched to your own special physique and style of shooting. This, as we already know, varies from one individual to the next — and that is the reason for **matching.** The tall, skinny people cannot necessarily shoot the same equipment that a stocky, short person can.

The bow should be considered first. It should be the right length for your draw. It should not be too long nor too short. A person with a short draw should have a bow short enough to make the recurves in the limb ends work enough to create the energy it was designed to produce. A person with a long draw should have the same thing; but since a short bow with a long draw would cause a drastic string angle on the fingers and pinch them, he should have a longer bow to reduce that pinch and still let the recurves perform as they should.

The draw weight of the bow should never be as much as you can pull. It is no secret that you can pull much more than you can control and shoot accurately. The draw weight should also be judged by how much **control** you have after you have shot two-thirds of the tournament. The last one-third may be when you need very positive control (not draw weight) to come out on top. Yes, I think you **should** shoot every pound that you can **control.** You and/or your coach could arrive at your maximum control-weight without too much trouble. It is very important that you do so.

Stay honest with yourself in your selection. Some of us shoot too light a bow because we are lazy or think we can't shoot a heavier one. Some of us shoot a bow that is too heavy because our ego sometimes is unreliable. If you are saddled with one pound more than you can control consistently, what have you gained? It is weight versus control.

Everything has its price.

The advantages of shooting all the draw weight you can control are speed, lower trajectory, less arrow time in the air, less magnification of mistakes and a cleaner release. All the draw weight you can control is also important and advantageous to you when shooting in the wind. Too heavy, too light, just right — who knows for sure, you ask? I say you and/or your coach, as well as the results you see when you try different things over a period of time, can give you that information.

The physical weight of the bow in the hand should again be no more than you can control, and I believe we should exercise to build up the muscles to better handle that most important part of shooting form, the bow and bow arm unit. I read someplace that there comes a point when the bow does not perform as well if it is too heavy in its mass weight. I do not know if that has been proven yet, but I agree.

To you, the shooter, as an individual, the grip on the bow handle is very important. Its size and shape contribute to and also take away from the success of your shooting. It does not make sense to me for a small-handed person to buy a bow with a big fat handle, or vice-versa. Most bow grips are good; the advancement in the interchangeable grip is a big help to the shooter, giving you another adjustment in fitting your equipment. Most shooters use the low wrist grip but some prefer the high wrist or the one between high and low. If the face of the grip is too flat, it could produce a lot more torque for **some** hands. If the face is too rounded, it will not be comfortable for some people. Find the grip that fits your style of shooting and your physique, then stay with it.

Arrows are a problem for a lot of people because they (the shooters) make it that way, or they let other people convince them they have a problem. Most of the time the problem is not the arrow. There is a great urge in all of us to think that whatever the good shooters use, that also is what we need; that is not necessarily so. What a good shooter uses is what he has matched up to fit himself as an **individual.**

There are a great number of shooters who can tune their own equipment and make it perform to a fine degree. However, there are far more shooters who do not make any effort whatsoever to learn how their equipment can be tuned to fit their physique and style, and they make no effort to have it tuned even if a good tuner is available.

Some areas have no one who knows how to perform this task. I know of one locality that has a good man, but, unfortunately, he will not tune for anyone else. I think it only fair also to mention that some localities have a friendly "expert" who will tune everything in sight.

By all means, you should have someone tune your equipment for you if you do not want to learn to do it yourself. (You can find lots of good information on the subject, and there are tuning articles in archery magazines from time to time.)

Building Blocks   7

There are people who are experts at tuning your equipment to fit you. Even if you have to travel a great distance, if you know a tuner who has a good reputation, make an appointment, spend some time and money, and get yourself set up right. It will be time and money well spent. By the way, a good, reliable, professional tuner will charge for his services. I would be more inclined to trust those who think their experience and know-how are worth something. It is pretty hard to go back to a "freebie" and complain.

Say you shoot today and are grouping A-OK. If you change nothing in your equipment and a week later shoot again, but your arrows wobble, for heavens sake **don't blame the equipment.** Check up on your form. Inconsistent form can make an arrow perform badly. That bow tuner has a most exasperating job trying to tune equipment for a shooter who has inconsistent shooting form. Get your form consistent and perfect it before you ask for a final tuneup job. If you want to be a good shooter, if you want to be better or want to make the team, by all means be sure that you are shooting equipment that is matched in **fit** and tuned to work right **for you.**

Victory has a thousand parents; defeat is an orphan.

Making one right shot

Winning archery is nothing more than one right shot, repeated time after time after time.

You want to shoot a certain score in a tournament or even in practice. The only way to get there is to shoot one shot at a time. Everyone knows that, but few realize and understand it.

I ask my students, "What are you shooting?"

The responses usually are, "This arrow," or "The third one," or "Poorly," or "Not too bad," etc.

The answer I'm looking for is, "This shot." Not this arrow. It's hard to get that point fully understood, that you're working only on one shot. You have to put it together only once. You shoot only one shot a tournament, and that's the one which is in the bow. That is the shot you have to put together.

With each shot, you begin again. It's a brand new ballgame. You don't come to shoot a tournament; you come to shoot one shot.

I stress that constantly. You **prepare the shot;** you don't just shoot an arrow. I want the shooter to feel the shot, know how it felt all through the preparation, explosion and follow through. I want you to feel it physically and mentally. You may not be able to do that at first, but eventually you will if you keep trying. At that stage, when you shoot a shot that is right, it

● *On the men's line at the 1976 Olympics, Darrell Pace, left, the eventual Gold Medalist, is at full draw and aiming as Richard McKinney mentally prepares his shot.*

is effortless and you really don't know what you did.

That shot felt a certain way. You can't explain how it felt, but you **know** how it felt. Consciously, you are feeling for the shot, and when you do that you are programming what that right shot feels like in your subconscious and your muscles. Then the subconscious will duplicate that. The brain won't need to give a command for those shots once you have the feel of it.

If you have difficulty with a shot while you're in practice or competition, you don't have to like it but you must accept it. If you accept that shot, then it is history. If the shot didn't feel good, and you know why, then you go ahead and fix the problem. If it didn't feel good, and you don't know why, then you just keep working for the right feel. Don't get hung up on "why" the bad shot occurred. A bad shot happens now and then, and you can't do anything about it.

And if the shot felt good, but didn't go where you felt it should have gone, accept it. You cannot become angry with the results of a shot which felt good. It is history and don't waste any more time with it. Just prepare the next shot. Do your best, relax, put it together and do it. If you get another good feeling and the shot goes where it was supposed to go, you've stayed on a positive plane.

If you don't remain positive, then you have to work harder. Remember, too, that some days you shoot and nothing seems to work. Those days will happen, and there isn't a thing you can do about them, except accept them and not get uptight about them. Some days, the wheels just spin.

There are things that could happen to you which you aren't aware of, and which could cause a bad release or some other thing. Say you slept soundly the night before, so soundly that you had lain on an arm without knowing it and that arm felt dead when you woke up. You had to rub it to regain good circulation and feeling in that arm. Who knows? Maybe that could cause a release problem later that day. Emotional problems, walled off in the back of your mind and supposedly forgotten could come back to cause a problem because they weren't dismissed as they should have been.

I don't want you to like errors or problems, but I sure don't want you to stand there on the line and dig back through your history to try to find out what may have caused them. That's what too many shooters want to do. They say, "But that's my weakness." That statement drives me up the wall. It's a cop-out.

You have to trust the feeling of a right shot. If it felt right, but you scored only a seven, you have to accept it and go on. If you'll just relax and believe in yourself, the problem probably won't occur again.

When you accept the results and understand them, then you're well on your way to believing. Believing is the big one. You must trust yourself and your preparation. You must trust that you will put the shot together properly. Then you will believe in yourself and believe the arrow is going in the gold.

Problems are funny. I was working with an outstanding shooter once. She believed her arrows would go in the gold, but once in a while one would hit about half an inch out at 10 o'clock. When I asked her why the odd arrow went out, she didn't know. She said she felt good with each shot, and it wasn't the same arrow every time.

I watched, and I couldn't see anything different. So I said, "You have some tension in your bow arm in that direction. I don't know which muscle it is, but you're not quite relaxed in your bow arm every time."

She never shot another arrow out of the gold that day.

Do you know what that says? That says she was accepting the odd arrow, when she shouldn't have. Her subconscious should have said, "Hey, I'm goofing up someplace."

She consciously didn't know what the problem was, but her subconscious did, and it made the correction.

You can't blame the arrow, but that's the first thing which usually happens. That's why I don't want shooters to use numbered arrows. The number gives them an excuse.

The top archers understand themselves . . . they understand what

---

You can't dwell on your blues or your failures. There is a syndrome in sports we call "paralysis by analysis." That means you spend so much time and energy analyzing your failure that you paralyze yourself.

Arthur Ashe

Building Blocks

they have to do . . . they understand their frailties . . . they accept what must be accepted, and they use it to become a positive. They don't worry about things needlessly. They have confidence and are secure.

Archery can be a lonely sport, but it shouldn't be

When you're standing at the line, you're on your own. There's no one to help you. Physically, it's passive, and that's what makes it so mental.

If you aren't in the habit of using your mind positively, to build confidence, trust and belief . . . then it's a lonely place up there at the shooting line. But if you have built all those positive things, then you're truly doing your best and you're not lonely because at that instance you don't need anyone. You are all that is necessary, and you know it.

Satisfaction, enthusiasm, fun = winning

Sometimes we get so all-fired wrapped up in the technical aspects of good shooting, and in preparing ourself to do our best, that everyone forgets to talk about enthusiasm, personal satisfaction and enjoyment. Without those elements, though, even if you shoot the highest score, how could you say you won?

The shooter so wrapped up in everything — whether or not he can control it — that he can't say good morning, doesn't really win. You can't get so wrapped up in the shooting and in yourself that it all becomes drudgery. You have to stay enthused. That will help your determination to do your best.

A machine has no feelings, no joy and no sadness either in that sense. A machine can't say to itself, "I gave it my best, and next time I'll try to improve on that."

You have to like competition. I teach that if you don't have any competition, you couldn't shoot. You should welcome competition. Even though you may be competing only against yourself, trying to do your best, it wouldn't be the same if you were the only person on the shooting line. You'd really have no way to test yourself, to find out whether all your work has paid off when it counts. Without the competition of other archers, you're not going to win nor are you going to have the satisfaction of doing your best. You want to prove to yourself that you've put it all together and can rise to your own challenges, but you also need to see just how well you do in the wider scheme.

Our society, unfortunately, too often makes us feel that if we shoot second, third, fourth or fifth, we haven't done anything. I don't agree with that. True, winning receives the recognition, but when the scores of the winner and the fifth place shooter are only a few points apart, it says a lot. Few people scored better than you if you're in one of those runner-up spots, and that is worth a certain amount of satisfaction.

Too many shooters don't get satisfaction out of anything but first place. A shooter with that attitude won't make first place, possibly because he isn't being honest with himself. A bridesmaid is a bridesmaid, but when you're in that position, you're certainly justified in saying, "Wait until next tournament." That's a positive outlook that will help you. Sometimes "almost, but not quite" can spur you on with greater determination.

No matter what the reason you're out there trying to do well, you have to enjoy it and find certain personal satisfactions. It can be a cold, tiresome place if you don't like the other people and wrap yourself in an impenetrable shell. The talk-fest which always takes place during and after shooting is as much a part of the total experience as is the shooting.

No one can make you feel inferior unless you agree with him.

If you have tried to do something and failed, you are vastly better off than if you had tried to do nothing and succeeded.

• The ultimate purpose of archery, or of any sport, is to enjoy yourself and the people you're with. When you do that, the rainy days are few and far between.

Chapter Two: Building and Keeping Mental Control

• *Olympic gold is a lofty goal. Darrell Pace and Luann Ryon reached that goal. For such an achievement, the heavy weight of gold, when suspended from a chain around the neck, is no weight at all.*

Set your goals

How should an archer set goals? Whatever way works for you individually.

It must be an **attainable** goal, otherwise you're setting yourself up for frustration and failure.

A student brought me up short a while back. I said to her, "I have no doubt that someday you will shoot a 1,300. I just don't know which day or which tournament."

"I don't want to shoot 1,300," she said.

That got my undivided attention.

"You what? Why not?" I sputtered.

"Because everyone wants to shoot 1,300," she said. "It's a number you can't reach. I want to shoot 1,320 when I do it."

Let me tell you, I learned from that. I don't encourage anyone anymore by telling them I know they can shoot 1,300. No, sir. I use 1306, 1307, 1308 . . . something like that.

The 1,300 score is a psychological barrier, just like the four-minute mile was a psychological barrier. Knowledgeable people used to give all sorts of reasons why the human body couldn't run a mile under four minutes, until Roger Bannister did it in 1954. Shortly after he broke the barrier, a whole bunch of guys did it. Somehow, an odd number isn't the psychological barrier. The more common number most people use seems to assume a strength of its own, and when we as individuals subscribe to that barrier, our group psyche holds us down as individuals.

How much practice is the right amount?

A coach can be a better coach if he listens.

I recall a group discussion I heard in regard to the amount of practice needed to stay in shape for best performance. I don't think what I am going to say here will have any effect on our best shooters, because in my opinion they already know all about what I think. They have found out what it takes (in practice) to perform their best and they know how to apply it. My purpose is to inform the uninitiated and the shooter who has not yet learned that he is a special individual who does things in an individual way for an individual reason. If he does anything in archery exactly like our best shooter, it quite possibly is a happenstance.

The group's discussion brought out several facts, one being that almost everyone (I think) really thought he did not practice enough. I would say they were unknowingly using that as an alibi for the way they were performing. Some, I am sure (because I know them) stretched a bit what they thought they put in, in daily practice. This (in my opinion) so they would (in their opinion) seem to be more in accord with the better shooter in the group who said he practiced a great deal. Some of the better shooters are very free with information on how much practice it takes to keep good, steady shooters shooting in top form, and they heartily endorsed (for everyone) the amount of time they spent at practice.

The guy who shoots below a good shooter thinks, "He must know what is good for me, because he shoots a better score than I do."

In this group was one of the best archers in the United States. I knew how much time that archer spends in practice just keeping in shape or preparing for an important tournament. I also know that this group had to ask this archer several times how much practice she does, how many hours a day, how much a week, a month. This archer was not trying to evade any question about practice, this archer stated very simply that it was whatever she felt she needed to get things feeling right and feel confident that she was performing as she should. No more or less. How do you really explain that to a group of eager beavers who want to do as you do because you do it?

This group did not really understand the real message she gave them, and they insisted until she made a guess at an average number of hours that she put in, in practice. I'm sure some are diligently following what they consider her method and are missing the true lesson she initially gave.

I have heard practice discussed in top national shooting groups. If they have to, and they generally do, they will put it into hours a day or hours a week, but they are all alike in that no two are alike in their needs or for that matter in how or how much they practice.

14

Mental Control

Let's get back to you, the individual who wants to know how many hours to practice to become a consistent top shooter and stay there. In my opinion, I cannot tell you, the man down the street cannot tell you, and the top shooter next door cannot tell you. I can say, however, that if you have a constant coach he can come the closest to telling you correctly. He can and will notice if you get carried away and practice so much you burn yourself out. He can and will tell you if you are goofing off and not sincere in your efforts. In my opinion, only **you** can correctly put the exact "how much" and "when" to the problem.

What am I trying to say? All of us know the basics of what we are doing. We know there are a lot of hours to put in. In practice, we know that we must keep at it to perfect form, to tone muscles, to get the feel of being organized, synchronized, stabilized, balanced and smooth.

We are not talking about the basic hours we put in to get the rough groundwork done. We are talking about (as I mentioned above) the amount of practice needed to stay in shape for best performance.

Don't ask me how much I practice and then copy it. Practice until you think perhaps you are getting groups that are too big, then rest or stop for a while. If you have a problem, work it out, but not on a basis of hours spent at it. Be honest with yourself. Don't use any excuses for work that needs to be done; call a spade a spade.

Listen to every Joe Blow but remember you are an individual, just as he is. Gather information from all sources, sift out what your common sense tells you to and investigate the rest for possible use to improve yourself.

Be a smart individual, use your brain and police yourself for the best there is in you.

A gauge of success is not whether you have a tough problem to handle, but whether it is the same problem you had yesterday.

When NOT to practice

There are times when you should **not** practice. I don't think you should practice when you're madder than the devil at someone, or if you're really physically ill. Don't practice any more than you have to; on the other hand, don't get so carried away with not practicing when you really don't want to that it becomes a lazy habit. That's when it becomes an excuse, and we know all about excuses, now, don't we.

At Joliette, Quebec, where the archery part of the 1976 Olympics was held, I had an interesting conversation. The tournament site was 43 miles from Olympic Village, and during practice days before competition we traveled by bus every day. All our archers usually slept on the way up and the way back.

When we'd reach the practice field, some of our archers would shoot maybe six shots, or 18 shots, or for four or five hours. It didn't matter, because we were there all day.

However, on the first day they just went out there and relaxed, just to get the feel of the place. Linda Myers shot quite a bit, but the others didn't. After they finished their shooting, they went out to a grassy area and tossed a frisbee. They had fun.

A couple of people were astounded. They asked why the kids weren't shooting.

"They don't want to," I said.

"They don't **want** to?"

"Nope."

"Why don't you make them practice?"

"Because it would be more harmful than helpful."

So I launched into an explanation of putting the shot together by how it feels, and the role confidence plays in good shooting, and how the individual shooters knew themselves well enough to know what they needed to do and didn't need to do, and they and I trusted each other and had confidence in their judgment. They were competitors and wanted to win; they also knew themselves well enough to know what to do to make themselves the best competitors.

They knew they didn't need to practice every day to keep the muscles tuned. In fact, you shouldn't either.

So maybe they'd horse around a while, then go back and shoot some more. Or maybe they would shoot for six hours the next day. Overall, they would shoot continually and carefully to keep their muscles tuned and their frame of mind right.

They knew that they were shooting fine, everything felt fine, the shots were going in . . . so why stand there and needlessly repeat it. They might overdo something, remove their eagerness to compete, at the very least. With too much shooting, they would have become tired and their groups would have opened up. Then their confidence would have slipped a notch, even if they hadn't felt it did.

Are your priorities and concentration right in practice?

Although we are supposed to practice so our accuracy will improve, how and what we practice is the key to how much, if at all, we improve. It does no good to put in hours of just flinging arrows and producing nothing except muscle flexibility. And even that can be negative if improperly applied.

I want to go on record as saying that nothing can or should replace practice; it is necessary in any sport, but it should be carried out with common sense and purpose.

Many times when I talk to archers about their shooting habits we have a conversation that goes something like this.

"When you practice, what are you really working on?"

"Well, trying to make my shooting better."

"What part of your shooting?"

"You know, standing, pulling, release — that sort of stuff."

"And at what distance do you practice the most?"

"Ninety meters."

"Why don't you practice at 30 meters?"

"Because I need more practice at the long distance."

"Why is it harder? What is different from shooting at 30 meters?"

"Well, it's further and I just have to be more careful when I shoot."

"Then when you move up to 70 meters you shoot better?"

"No, not always and that's what bugs me."

"What do you think is the reason you don't shoot better when the target is 20 meters closer?"

"That's what bugs me."

"How about 50 meters? How do you do there?"

"Well, the face gets smaller and that bothers me some, but I generally do pretty well at 30 meters."

Let's talk about the above questions and answers.

Question One — A great many people put in a lot of time on the practice butts just shooting, but just shooting is not enough. You can strengthen the muscles, but if they don't know what they are supposed to do, you will never get the results you want on the target face.

Time and practice with a purpose is not just standing, pulling and releasing. It is a concentrated effort, knowing exactly how the shot feels and why it feels that way. It's knowing when the feel is right and when the feel is not right.

Question Two — There are many reasons why it is important to practice at the longer distances. No one takes issue with that, but it is also important to practice at all the other distances as well.

Are you really supposed to be more careful about how you shoot at the long distances than you are at the short ones? I don't think so. The name of the game is consistency. You won't get that 100 percent if you are more careful at one distance than you are at another.

I don't think the long distance is harder to shoot than any other distance. It depends on what you think when you say "shoot." Everyone asks how you shot. What they want to know is your score.

I always shoot my best for that day, but sometimes my score is not too impressive.

Mental Control

How you shoot is your performance, both physical and mental, for that day, that tournament. What you scored is the result of how you shot. When you learn how to prepare yourself, through practice, your scores will be higher.

Question Three — Too many archers shoot a lower score at 70 meters than they do at 90 meters. Why?

There are many reasons.

One of those is the fact that the shooter discovers he is shooting well above his average at 90 meters and he sees he has a chance to rack up his highest score ever and it scares the devil out of him. He quits thinking, or has never trained himself to think, and he tightens up, tries too hard and can't relax.

The same can be true for a bowhunter who finds himself looking at the biggest whitetail deer he has ever seen.

The opposite of that is the guy who is more careful at 90 meters. He practices being careful at 90 meters, so now 70 meters is a piece of cake. He is in the habit of not trying so hard at 70 meters, so when he slacks off in his efforts his scores slack off at the same time.

There is no substitute for being careful, regardless of the distance you are shooting from.

Never go to practice unless you intend to bear down hard and work at what you're doing. Having fun with the gang is fine if that's as far as you want to go, but don't get upset if your scores aren't always number one.

Somewhere, I read that people who want to win are a dime a dozen. I want people who want a chance to prepare to be winners.

Shooting form is like a jigsaw puzzle — big pieces and little pieces. The longer you shoot, the smaller the pieces get.

Are you gaining on it?

How do you know you're making headway when the scores don't show it?

Good question. Tough one, too. Nothing frustrates me more than seeing a shooter with beautiful, practically flawless form scoring less than he or she should in a tournament. The shooter looks like he brought it all with him, but there's something missing.

I realize this almost seems the reverse of the question, but hang with me, I'm getting to it.

You have to forget about score. You have to work on the building blocks, developing the feel, or whatever. You have to be realistic and realize that your arrows are going where they are in the target because you put them there. The sight wasn't wrong; the sight is never wrong. The sight always gets those arrows going in the direction you point them. You may have set the sight wrong, that's all.

Or the arrow is located in the target in some less-than-desirable location because of something you did back in the form, in putting the shot together.

One of the best ways of making headway when it doesn't look like you are is to be certain you keep your priorities in order. That will keep you realistic on a step by step basis. If you lose track of the things you must do to put together one perfect shot, or if you're afraid to back up and work on some of those elements, then you're not going to go where you profess you want to go. It's as simple as that.

Everything which happens that you don't like, you did it. You have to realize that, but not condemn yourself for it. Too many people condemn themself for a little mistake. Or a big mistake.

You must **accept** that mistake and go on. If you make that mistake three or four times, then you're being rather dense and ought to be mad at yourself, but once is no big thing. And if you're working on something which may be hard to learn, making mistakes isn't anything. You have to make those mistakes to learn.

Obstacles are those terrible things you see when you take your eyes off the goal.

Never think 10 (heresy, heresy!)

I used to tell you that you should try to shoot 10's. I coached that you should always strive to put the arrow in the center.

Not any more. I don't mention 10's, nor do I mention the center of the target.

I believe that that viewpoint helps breed target panic. It tries to get you to aim finer than you can; it makes you strive too hard.

In addition, it produces only acceptable or negative results. It can never produce a better than acceptable result. It does not allow you to reward yourself when you exceed expectations.

Now, I talk about nines or the gold. I'd rather say yellow than gold, because we're all conditioned to think "perfect" or "10" when we think gold. And then we try too danged hard.

I've proven, to my satisfaction, that the system works.

A couple of years ago, during a conversation with one of my students, he told me that at 90 meters he told himself that he must get all his arrows in the red (which would be a seven or eight on the FITA face).

I asked why the devil he didn't tell himself that he wanted to get them all in the nine. "Do you realize what your score would be if you got all your arrows in the nine ring?," I asked him.

"No. I haven't really thought of it."

"You'd have a 1,296."

"Wow!"

"But you're on the right track, trying to put them all in the red at least, not trying to put them all in the center."

So he tried that a while . . . shooting for the gold and nines. Presently he came clear across the field from where he had been shooting to where I was still coaching.

"You know, that works," he said. "I'm shooting better groups."

The more I thought about it, the more I could see that you can get uptight when you don't get a 10 or feel that you can't hold the pin in the center.

Then I asked a few shooters "If you had all your arrows in the gold, at least a nine, how many do you think would find their way into the 10?"

"At least half," they said.

Ok, that's an added 72 points. Add that to 1296 and you get 1,368. Nobody's shot that yet. Haven't even come close.

Well, let me tell you, that made as much of an impression on me as it did on my shooters. To think that you can get 1,296 and still have a reasonable chance of going way above that . . . that's inspiring. The nine-ring sort of becomes like par in golf — it's danged good, but when everything's clicking you can do even better. That's positive all the way, and it is encouraging.

You cannot imitate success. You have to create it.

● Len Cardinale, left, well-known coach of pro and amateur champions, and Al Henderson, two long-time friends, in a little over-the-fence talk.

100 percent concentration for conscious and subconscious control

The fascinating thing about archery is that it is an individual effort all the way. Although you are on the shooting line with 50 other people, you are all alone, isolated from everything and everybody. You stand or fall, depending upon how much you, **and only you,** control the shooting effort.

Unfortunately, a great many shooters never realize this. The control needed to shoot a good shot is not easy to come by. The importance must first be understood by the shooter, and then through practice and experience under pressure be perfected to a degree that will produce the scores that are desired.

Many things can plague you in your effort to get good control.

In this respect, I see a fantasy. I think perhaps there is a little devil who likes to stand by, waiting until we make the first wiggle toward a mistake. He helps us lose confidence, get discouraged, feel sorry for ourselves and post a poor score. He loves his job and works hard for those who say, "The devil made me do it." He is there **only** because we **allow** him to be there.

On the other side, there is a little angel who is also ready and willing to help us put it all together, give us confidence, forgive our mistakes and help us stay happy and relaxed. She compliments us on our sincere efforts, helps us accept what we are doing today and improve it tomorrow. This little angel is our friend and tells us that the little devil's way may seem easier, but it won't produce what we want in a tournament. She also is there because we **allow** her to be there.

We have a choice. Which one will we listen to, the devil or the angel?

Control of a good shot is made easier if everything leading up to and including the explosion and the follow-through is prepared as it should be. There are thousands of arrows shot by hundreds of archers who just pull up, anchor, aim and let 'er go, because they are not aware that an archer preparing a shot is like a watchmaker preparing to make a fine watch so it will run and keep perfect time. Each small part and detail of the watch must be assembled by a craftsman who is meticulous in his efforts to make each one perfect.

Preparing the shot is, of course, a controlled effort, but there is a finer point here that I want to bring out. Preparing the physical part of the shot is more or less a conscious effort — and can be such — until you are ready to aim. At this point, it should then become a subconsciously controlled effort while you mentally concentrate upon the important task of aiming.

Let's go completely through a shot.

First, you must have equipment that is set up and tuned especially **for you,** equipment that will fit your style of shooting. Tried and true equipment that you know and believe in completely. Neither should it be set up like anyone else has his or her tackle set and tuned, unless it has proven to be right for you and your style of shooting. It must be your equipment, set up for you and accepted by you.

Whenever you are ready to actually start the preparation of a shot, keep this in mind — you must **complete** the **physical** set up of your form **before** you ever think about aiming. Remember that — **before you aim.**

Step up to the shooting line and consider your stance, the position of your hand on the bow and your fingers on the string, how tight or loose you consistently anchor, which muscles to use, when and how you should pull and how you hold.

Now **relax, hold** and see how you **feel.** If you have prepared everything correctly, you should know it. The feel will be right. You may **now aim.**

At this point, you must turn over completely the control of this physical part of the shot preparation, as I have called it, to your subconscious mind and trust it to do what it has been trained to do. You must do this without any conscious or unconscious interference whatsoever, while you mentally and consciously concentrate upon aiming. You will, however (as in hypnotism), always retain the conscious knowledge that if, at any point, control of the physical effort, as it then is, is subconsciously rejected, you will let the shot down and prepare it all over again correctly. Then you are free to devote your conscious effort again to the all-important task of aiming.

This part of preparing a shot is the least understood, **but the most critically important,** of the preparedness effort. I think a good shooter can and will put 100 percent of his concentration into aiming. He should try to constantly project a ray of concentration dense enough to burn a hole through the center of the target. Not for one fleeting part of a second should he think of anything else, until after the explosion and the completion of the follow-through.

With or without a clicker, there is no problem getting rid of the arrow. The explosion will trigger at the right time. You must not think about how or when to cause the explosion.

This principle of preparing a shot, if you haven't tried it, needs to be thought through and then practiced.

Any serious shooter can practice, under pressure, this kind of control until it is firmly engraved upon his subconscious mind. It will then become an effortless habit.

You can consciously put together the first and basic part of your physical form and then practice turning over that part of your preparedness to your subconscious while you consciously bring all of your mental

Mental Control

powers together and concentrate on aiming at the center of your target. Your sweetest, easiest, most perfect shot is when you have to ask someone if the shot really did go off. That's concentration on aiming, with an automatic trigger.

The little devil is cute, but the little angel is your pal; let her help **you control** what **you** put together.

How to handle mistakes

How do you handle mistakes? You accept them.

I ask my students, "Do you want to win?"

"Yeah," they say.

"Well then, you'd better start making some mistakes and accepting them," I reply. A coach heard me say that once and looked at me like I'd gone crazy. But I haven't.

When we were babies in cribs, we learned simply by doing things. There was no critical evaluation one way or the other. We just did things and learned and were encouraged by each newly learned thing, even if it was just learning to roll over.

Then we grew a few years and were playing on the lawn. A neighbor kid comes over and suddenly you're both going after the same ball tossed across the lawn. He passes you, and then is when you start noticing there is competition. Along with that comes a natural worry that maybe you've done something wrong, and you think that was why he outran you. That's when you really start the learning process.

If your parents handle it right, you learn that somebody might be better than you at a certain thing, that this fact isn't a tragedy, and that you always do the best you can but there's nothing wrong if you don't win. We might not do something well or right the first time we try something, but we'll keep trying and sooner or later we'll understand and do it right. We keep the positive outlook.

That is why it is not right to coach for perfection. We are fallible. We have to accept that. We can try to improve, but trying to be perfect sets an impossible, ultimately negative goal.

How to whip the wind at its own game

Are you one of those archers who can't shoot well in the wind? Do you feel that although you have been shooting well for some time, in the wind you can never seem to put it together just right?

Perhaps you are misunderstanding something, but don't feel too badly — when it's windy, you'll have lots of company at any tournament. If 50 shooters are there, 40 will have told everyone else several times why they are not shooting very well that day.

"That damned wind" is causing it.

I think they are barking up the wrong tree. Very few shooters will ever stop and think that this windy handicap is playing no favorites. It is blowing on everyone else, too. Oh, **you** might get a gust now and then, but it had to come from where **he** is and will go on to where **she** is and will even out about the same, so what is all the griping about?

In my opinion, this is a made-to-order situation for those shooters who are in need (habit) of some excuse to account for their poor shooting. They are really glad for a windy day, because the excuses they usually use are getting rather transparent. A windy day is a crackerjack explanation that seems believable.

Some of the more hardy ones even use a windy day as an excuse for not attending a tournament. They think everyone else will understand that windy tournaments "bug" them. (Everyone else couldn't care less.) Some will go to the tournament knowing they never score very well in a wind, but they know and understand the reasons, so they hang in there and **shoot** very well.

Perhaps you think that I am being facetious, but I am not. You can prove it. At the next three tournaments you attend, make a mental note of every negative reason you hear for poor shooting. By the third tournament, you will begin to recognize more and more of the negative excuses people use, and you will be able to understand what those excuses really are. If you approach this experiment with an open mind, you also will begin to see and understand that you yourself are using some pretty silly excuses.

This experiment should also wake you up to the fact that no one gives a tinker's damn why you don't shoot well that day. It should be obvious, then, that you are only psyching yourself down with negative thoughts about your ability to shoot. This will insure that you will shoot a lower score that day.

The next time you are plagued by a low score because you shot poorly on a windy day, how about trying to understand that what you are saying and believing may not be the truth? It seems to me the truth is your **score** is the only thing that is messed up.

The point I am trying to make is that the word **score** and the word **shoot** do not mean the same thing. **Shoot** and **score** are not synonymous. Your form determines the way you shoot, good or bad. The wind determines the way you score, high or low. Using the word **shoot** to explain a poor **score** in the wind may be condemning the best **form** on the shooting line.

When you say you can't shoot well in the wind, I interpret that to mean that your form goes to pot when the wind blows. Most of the time, if it does it is only because you have convinced yourself it will. I see no reason for your form to change from good to poor just because the wind is blowing.

Mental Control

Lower scores? Yes.

Bad form? For what reason? Yes, the wind blows you around some and it is harder to hold your aim. In what way, though, did the wind make you prepare your shot any differently?

Think about this: If your shot is prepared right . . . if your concentration is 100 percent . . . if the follow-through is A-OK, then, for gosh sake, you can shoot good in any wind.

Have faith in your ability to shoot well. **Prepare** your shots as you always do. **Execute** the shot as you always have. **Aim** the best you can, as you always try to do, and accept the fact that the wind will probably cause your (and everyone else's) score to be lower. Shoot well and let only the wind be the reason that your score is lower than usual — if it is lower.

I learned a lot in 1938, when we used to shoot with a bunch of archers from Pitcher, Oklahoma. If the wind was blowing, they would beat us every time. Seems that windy days were all they ever had. The best advice I ever got about wind shooting came from a guy they called Porter.

Never try to force the bow arm to stay still, he said. Just let it float, and if the wind pushes it past the bull, just float it back. The wind will try to win, but you must be smarter than it is.

Wish I knew where ol' Porter was today. I'd like to thank him again for that sage bit of advice.

If you're having trouble, analyze yourself to determine the source of the lack of control.

Questions can provide the best answers

I don't think we can succeed very well at anything unless we get into the habit of thinking, using common sense and remembering (under pressure) what we have learned from the hard knocks of experience.

When coaching, I want to establish in the student the habit of thinking on every question before the student acts. These questions need not be asked by someone else. In fact, what we must understand is that we ask ourselves questions all the time, and unless we have the habit of **thinking** what the answer **could** be, we will be working our heads off trying to improve our relationship with our subconscious self, but getting nowhere.

Questions can be very simple and still not be answered correctly. Some can be tricky (if you like that word). All should be thought over before they are answered.

Which is most important, the SPEED of the bow or the accurate CONTROL of the shot?

Well, gee whiz, that was an easy one, but would you like to guess how many speed demons would answer speed if they were asked that question? Yes, there are some who want their bows like their cars — too hot to handle. That is just what happens. You can find those archery people down at the end of the target line and the car people in the obituary column. Nothing takes the place of control except the lack of it. If you can't control, you have a problem to tackle.

Is there any reason or advantage to pulling your low scoring arrows from the target first and your high scoring arrows last?

Psychologically, I think there is. It may be small and unimportant to some people, but when you combine that with all the other little things we do to boost our confidence, it could be worth two points in a tournament. Those two points could mean a win, or perhaps a record, that day.

If you pull an arrow from the outside ring last, that is the image implanted in your mind of where those arrows were. To you, that is a negative picture to cope with.

I never let anyone pull my arrows from the target face because I want to go back to the shooting line with the picture in my mind's eye of my arrows coming out of the gold or bullseye. That will give me a mite more confidence.

When you leave the target, close your eyes and see what the picture is.

When an arrow lands in the wrong scoring area, what does that tell you?

You could say that the thing just took off. You know better, but the arrow might be crooked. The guy behind you belched and you flinched. The wind took a notion to blow. You almost have a blister and it bothers you some.

Answers like that are used every day, but the real answer is a simple one. **You did not prepare the shot correctly. You lost control.** If you think it was the wind, the man behind you or the blister, then you are not facing up to the facts of shooting. If that question does not tell you something, then **you** are not thinking.

When your bow sight is wrong, what should you do?

The sight, in my opinion, is **never** wrong. **You** may have it set in the wrong place to hit the 10. It may be too high, too low, too far right or left, but how could that inanimate little thing be wrong? That would be a negative thought of the first order. That's about the best sabotage you could ever think up for your subconscious.

How could you ever aim with any confidence if you once thought your sight was wrong? If you think it could be wrong, then no matter where you set it, you wouldn't have the confidence to accept it. You couldn't change it and believe that the adjustment would put the arrow in the 10-ring. No matter where you set it, your subconscious mind would reject the idea because it has been trained that when a sight is wrong, it is wrong. You can tinker with it all you want and get nowhere. You should train yourself to believe that your sight is never wrong. Then you will always be able to shoot where the sight is set. That may not be where you want the arrow to hit, but you can adjust the sight to fix that.

At the state tournament, a friend thought your bow was braced too low so he loaned you another string, which brought the height up where he thought it should be. Would you do the same for him?

I saw this done not too long ago, but I don't know if the guy ever returned the favor or not. Some would, I guess. Some would not. In my opinion, no friend would ever do a thing like that for you unless you specifically asked him to do it.

There are people who do not know everything, and they are sometimes preyed upon by those who **think** they know everything. The point is that the archer (in spite of his low string) had sight settings, was shooting his average and had confidence. Now, nothing is working, his confidence is shot and he has a problem. It could be that his friend(?) was a close competitor, smart enough to help him lose. It has been done.

Are you honest with that person in the mirror?

I come in contact with every kind of average-score archer you could possibly dig up, and I have come to some rather unsettling conclusions on why many archers are mediocre and why they remain mediocre.

Let me hit you with one of the conclusions that really sets most lukewarm shooters on their ear: They are liars!

I know that you are going to read the rest of this article just to see how many other stupid remarks I'm going to make. But before you judge my remarks in their entirety, let's get serious about that statement.

These shooters are upright, solid citizens, truthful, honest and respected by all who know them. They wouldn't deliberately tell you a falsehood, yet they lie to themselves every time they pick up a bow and attend a tournament.

A lot of archers have no real intention of getting above mediocrity. They say they do, and may think they do, but when they get right down to it they won't give the extra effort **and honesty** needed to get up higher.

Such shooters are not to be confused with the people who have fun shooting, enjoy the sport and the people, but have no intention of winning. They are honest with themselves and their limitations of the moment, and they usually end up improving just because they're not lying. They work as hard as they want, or as little as they want, and if some little part of their form or equipment setup improves, they're happy with the results.

Some people know they are lying to themselves and don't want to get past mediocrity. Verbally, they say they want to improve, but they don't. Those shooters I can't really feel sorry for, even though I will do my darnedest to help solve their problems when they ask. These poor devils who are lying to themselves and don't realize it are the ones who deserve any special help you can give them.

Not very many shooters, however, appreciate anyone (even their paid coach) telling them what they are doing to themselves. And some just won't believe it. I guess it does take guts to admit even to yourself that you are guilty of the crime when there are so many nice, easy, plausible things to blame the mediocre shooting onto. Such a shooter will not accept the truth and will go to great lengths to not accept it.

The coach knows the problem, and he knows what you are capable of. He understands why you stay mediocre and what will put you up in a better class. He will beat his brains out trying to make you understand that truth, that admission of fact, but only your true desire to improve will put you where you want to go.

There is a difference between knowing what is wrong and accepting it, and knowing what is wrong and not accepting it. And that difference, in the latter condition, is the lack of willingness to honestly face a problem and then work to solve it.

Too many mediocre archers want to go from here to 20 points better tomorrow, without working. They figure lessons or new equipment will suddenly make them better. The work factor is forgotten; the shooter lies to himself.

Everyone should get in the habit of listening to and talking to all the shooters that are most always on target one, if at all possible, especially at the regional and national level. I have yet to hear those people telling themselves a big lie as a reason for a poor arrow or poor round. They tell it like it is; they are interested in facts and they face those facts even when those facts say they, themselves, made the mistakes. They are on target one; they do what it takes to stay there, with no pussyfooting around. They have a lot of honest desire to be there, and they're willing to accept what it takes to get there.

It is simple, but not easy.

Put the blame where it belongs — on **you.** Your tackle is tuned, or it should be. Admit and understand that your sight is never wrong; it may be set wrong to hit the bullseye, but it shot where you held it. Understand and admit that your bow is not shooting low; it is shooting where

28   Mental Control

you put it. Understand and admit that those big trucks going by don't bother you; **you allow them** to bother you.

It is no secret that the smallest sights, sounds, feelings or thoughts are recorded in our subconscious mind. Now, that subconscious mind does not know the difference between right and wrong (and I don't mean morally). It records what we feed it — lies or facts — and lies can become facts to us.

I have been talking about lies you use against yourself to keep from facing reality.

However, there is a form, not really of lying but of stretching the truth, which can have a good effect. This is the truth you stretch when something needing correcting in your form feels a little bit improved on a shot — but you tell yourself that it felt quite a bit better. You really make a positive issue of it, build it up and make yourself feel good. You burn it into your muscles and brain.

This is the power of positive thinking. This is optimism and proper attitude. You tell yourself you're getting better, begin believing you're getting better, and you will do just that.

Your technique will improve because it is now easier to work on and work harder at it. The **emphasis is upon yourself.** You say "I'm getting better." This is the guts to try something, to fix something because you have the confidence to do it and want to do it. You compliment the person who beat you today, but you say under your breath, "Watch out, Mac."

So ask yourself, "Am I really lying to myself? Have I been less than honest?"

If you understand and apply the proper attitude and honesty, you will acquire that commodity which puts people on top. It's called **confidence in yourself.**

Strangely, or maybe not so strangely, the person who poo-poos this commentary the most is the one most in need of it. That gives an indication of how difficult it is to be honest with yourself. But it can be done. The winners do it.

If you are not big enough to stand criticism, you are too small to be praised.

Garth Henrichs

Dedication pays the dues

As a participant in archery, do you ever dream about outshooting the entire world someday? I suppose we all have our dreams of showing the world how great we are, but some individuals leave their dreams where

● Earl Hoyt, master bowyer and friend of amateur archery throughout the world, in a discussion with Al Henderson during some foul weather. Rick McKinney is listening in.

● Talking over a dream, a goal, Al Henderson and John Kazak, a top U.S. amateur archer, check a couple of things in the pursuit of excellence on the archery range.

Mental Control

they found them — to die for want of further attention. Others will pursue the dream half-heartedly and arrive nowhere. A small percentage will want that dream to come true, and will be so determined to see it happen they'll take out after it and make it become reality.

I don't think it's crazy for anyone to dream about becoming an international champion on the target field or the best bowhunter in the woods. The competition is wide open, and all you have to do is decide you want the dream badly enough to dedicate all your effort toward understanding what you have to do to earn it, accept whatever sacrifices you must make and then go after it.

If you convince yourself that you'll never realize your dreams, you'll be right. If you can convince yourself that you, as an individual, have as good a chance as anyone else, then it can become a reality.

I don't think any top shooter or hunter has a mystic power over equipment, targets or game that will help him or her shoot more accurately than anyone else. As top shooters, they're no more intelligent, better looking, richer, poorer, luckier or unluckier than you are. Anything they can do, you can do.

I'm convinced that champions in any sporting field have no more brains than the rest of us; however, they make better use of their time and talents than most of us do. They are definitely more dedicated to their dream goals of a national championship or Pope and Young deer and they prove it by putting pressure on themselves. They like a challenge, welcome it and thrive on it. They're smart enough to know that if they want to do their best they must have the competition to push them to a greater effort. They're dedicated to take the time to produce better than good form and mental control of that form. The hours of practice they do each day is a labor of love. They won't always win, but they're realistic enough to understand and accept that fact. They believe in themselves and their ability to perform well at whatever they set out to do. They are the individuals who grab their bow, find the toughest competition around and take pride in themselves regardless of the outcome, because they know they gave it their best that day.

Does the above description scare the socks off you and make you wonder what you're doing in this sport of kings? Shame be upon you if it does. Some people have a natural talent for doing things, and it appears easy for them to perform specific tasks. But how about those people who learn to do the impossible things after they become handicapped? We call that guts and fortitude. Everyone has it, we just have to decide to use it.

Remember, the wind blows, the cold rain falls and the hot sun shines on champions no matter who they are or what trophy they may be after. They know the wind, rain and sun play no favorites and that you are getting your share too.

Mental Control   31

I don't know of anyone who would not like to beat champions and be known as the best, but there may be some who, because of other responsibilities, know they do not have the time to accomplish it. Please note that I said "the time" to work toward victory. Anyone who shoots even one arrow has no excuse not to try to improve his shooting skills. It doesn't matter where they are in the scheme of things, but it does matter what they do while they are there. If they aren't shooting for pleasure, why are they shooting? Pleasure increases when we improve what we are doing.

Take a look at yourself and your dream goals. Ask yourself where you really want to go, put the facts on the line and look at them. Be fair with yourself but also be tough enough to admit your weaknesses. Decide how to become the new you and commit yourself to a campaign of improvement.

If you keep your foot on first base, you can't steal second base. All progress requires risk.

Confidence is the key to winning

A lot of people who shoot target archery have the potential to be world-class shooters. They're strong, they have the time to practice, and they exhibit almost flawless physical form. Yet they never seem to be able to put all the things together that should produce the kind of scores they're capable of shooting.

Upon observing the effort such shooters put into refining their form, as well as the perfection of their release and follow-through, you'd expect that the groups they shot would be tight and in the right place. When they aren't, there has to be a reason why the group isn't tight and in the center.

People say there's a reason for everything, and I agree with them. They also say there's more than one way to do something, so let's explore some possible solutions which might help those who are always bridesmaids and never brides.

In everything we do, an option exists which will produce the best, most consistent results with less time and effort. Quite often it involves the simplest of things. Nevertheless, it still depends upon the individual's contribution (or lack of it) when the time comes to put that option to use.

Unconsciously, some shooters always try to come up to somebody else's expectations, never knowing exactly what those expectations are and, as a result, never reaching the level of performance they themselves can be proud of.

If you feel you have to explain or apologize to anybody because a day crops up when, try as you will, nothing seems to come together as you'd like it, stop and think — just whom are you shooting for?

Who is the most important person at that precise time in your game? Whom do you really owe allegiance to? **It should be you.** Who else really cares one little bit about how you're shooting or what your score is?

You're right — **you** care, and you should. How in the world can you be embarrassed at what you're doing when you're doing the very best you can at that time? You **should** be embarrassed if you let down or quit. I'd be embarrassed for you, too. However, I'd support any score you might shoot as long as you have pride in yourself and strive to please only the person doing the shooting.

I realize you might like to please your Uncle Henry, but you don't owe him or anyone else for the way you shoot or your final score, providing that you've given it your best.

Another robber of high scores (when the physical form looks perfect) is a lack of complete concentration on the right thing at the time of the release-explosion. The importance of perfect execution during and **after** the explosion is something that only a select few understand and practice regularly. Everyone knows what concentration is, but not so many know how or when to use it. When practicing on some special part of your form, concentrate on it until it's implanted securely in your subconscious mind and it becomes a habit.

When you get into competition, trust everything you've prepared in practice to operate on its own, without any last-second interference from your conscious mind. Then, concentrate 100 percent on the place where you **believe** the arrow will appear on the target face. That concentration must continue, without a break, until the arrow gets there.

I believe that those who have "perfect" form and never seem to score well don't concentrate on anything after the mind gives the command to release the arrow. Their minds are turned off at the most critical moment — the split second that encompasses the release, the flight of the arrow, and its impact upon the target face.

They generally don't believe that, but they could prove it for themselves if they wanted; all they have to do is observe the top shooters.

Study the top shooters yourself. Notice their concentration until their arrows hit — every one of them. Notice that they don't apologize for a poor score or explain it away. They're trying to beat you, not please you. They ask no favors and expect none. They buy, with blood, sweat and tears, any advantage they may have over their competition.

They accept their mistakes as reminders to keep the pressure on themselves to perfect what they already have. Anything less than that would put them where they refuse to go.

As I've said before, most people don't realize just what they're capable of. You, as a shooter, and even in the rest of your life, should ask yourself whether your performance suffers because you're worrying about proving something to somebody other than yourself. Also check, very honestly, if, when, and how much you really concentrate. You might be surprised at the difference it makes.

When you want more, make yourself worth more.

Are you doing what you're supposed to be doing or what you think you're doing?

Today I asked my wife Violette (three-time Arizona state champion) what she thought was the hardest thing a shooter had to conquer to become a champion or even a good shooter.

Although I had no idea what her answer to my question would be, she fooled me by saying something that brings up a question which touches on both the physical and mental aspects of shooting — hard to explain so everyone can profit from it, hard to understand because it takes a heap of thinking to analyze the words and make constructive sense out of them.

She said she thought the hardest thing an archer had to learn to conquer was to be able to know whether he **was** or whether he **was not** doing what he **thought** he was doing.

Now just how do you go about knowing if you **are** doing or **are not** doing what you **think** you are doing?

A word of caution — please do not confuse what we are saying here. We are not saying, "How do you know if you **are** or **are not** doing what you are **supposed** to be doing?" We can make the same mistake in reading as we might in shooting and swear that we read **supposed** to be doing instead of **think** we are doing. There is a big difference.

No one does this kind of thing with a premeditated effort. It just seems to slip up on the best of us, and we are then hard pressed to believe it happened, no matter how we find out we are not doing what we thought we were.

If you have a good coach — and I am a firm believer in the need for one because he can catch something you may be doing wrong before it becomes a deep-seated habit — that coach can see and understand that you are not doing what you think you are. He can help **you** understand what to do to fix it.

As I said before, if you have a good coach, you have the problem licked, up to a point. Where that point comes is reflected by the amount of trust you put in that coach, how much you believe what your coach says and then, of course, the amount of labor you are willing to exert toward improvement.

No coach is worth very much to you unless you have faith in what he is trying to do for you and wholeheartedly work with him. Faith and believing are two key words to answering our question.

Sixteen-year-old Ellen, when told by her coach that she was four inches short of pulling the string to her chin, said, "I do pull it to my chin." She was honest; she thought she did.

Fifteen-year-old Blaine said, "I don't care what you see; I do not do it that way." He too was honest; he thought he didn't.

Ellen listened and believed and is now near the top in competition. Blaine would not listen or believe. He quit archery completely.

It matters not whether you are told by someone else that you are not doing what you think you're doing or whether, on your own, you have a sneaking feeling that it is true. The fact remains that you must **believe** that it **could be so.** You should be flexible enough and honest enough with yourself to check it out, prove it if possible and attempt to put it together some other way.

If you are working alone or with someone, your mental job is to teach yourself to feel the difference between what you **are** doing and what you **think** you are doing.

It is sort of a trial-and-error method. Perhaps it is more like a sixth sense that tells you to stop, look and listen.

It is a feeling, a hunch, a premonition that your unconscious self is sensing and trying to tell you about. Your job is to learn to tune in well enough to hear it when it wants to talk to you.

It does not matter how it comes to you; what does matter is that you teach yourself to recognize it when it manifests itself. Train yourself to use every bit of cunning that you possess to ferret out any discrepancies in what you **think** you are doing over what you **actually are** doing.

The key words here are **mental discipline.**

If all that sounds very complicated, it is not necessarily so. We are talking about any human being who has trained diligently and is so well-tuned to himself and to the operation at hand that he can and does do what seems like an impossible feat.

It is not impossible. You can do everything we have talked about. If you think all this is just for a very select group, join that group.

Handling t-t-t-target p-p-p-panic

Whenever I'm asked, "What is target panic?" I get the feeling that we have a problem.

When a student asks, "How do you get rid of it if you get it," I'm sure we have a problem.

It's not that I don't know what target panic is or how to stop it, but the problem is so individual and psychological that I feel inadequate when I try to explain what I believe. But here are my thoughts.

What is target panic? If you want to keep it simple, you can say it is a lack of self control on your part.

How do you get target panic? You develop a fear, knowingly or unknowingly, of something that has not yet happened.

How do you cure target panic? Simply stated, you must overcome your fears, whatever they are, with restored confidence.

How do you tell what those fears are? What they are or might be is not as important as recognizing that they are eroding your confidence, which destroys your control.

How do you get your confidence back? Have an honest faith in yourself and your abilities. Single out the most important thing to do and then work and work and work at it.

Target panic manifests itself to the conscious mind when you discover that you cannot execute your shot sequence the way you want. You get hung up somewhere in the process. You can't fully draw, you shoot too soon, you can't release, you can't aim. You feel foolish, you get mad and you start slugging.

I once had target panic so bad, I thought I invented it. At one point, I tried to give up archery because of it. I think that I can best convey my message to you by describing how I defeated my target panic.

Whatever my fears were, I could not put the pin on the "X." If I forced it, everything else went to pot and I looked stupid. My common sense told me I was acting ridiculous. The more I forced the worse it got. I tried tricks and, boy, I had some dandies. I felt foolish, embarrassed and picked on. I got disgusted. I cussed, got mad and got not one bit better.

I finally realized that my subconscious self was at war with my conscious self. Since I am supposed to be responsible for what my subconscious self thinks, I needed to exert some control over it. To do that, I had to understand that I had to overcome my subconscious objections (fears) every time I drew an arrow.

I should not be afraid to fail, or to make a mistake while trying to succeed. That meant everything else that I thought important must be pushed aside — pride, embarrassment, my ego, etc. Nothing must interfere with the control I needed to do what I was afraid to do.

I attended large and small tournaments, and I shot with only one thought in mind: I must **win** over my subconscious fears by **aiming,** no matter how sloppy or unorthodox my form looked. In many tournaments, I completely missed the butt more than 20 times out of 90 shots, and that can make a grown man cry.

I took a lot of abuse from friends and from my own pride, but I gloried in the fact that as bad as it looked on the outside, I was on my way to

Mental Control

winning on the inside.

I finally re-educated my subconscious self and made it back up to target number one, but only because my values had been sorted out and rearranged. I made it because I was now **not afraid to fail.** I was not afraid to make a mistake.

Target panic is not something to be ashamed of, and it is not something to blame yourself for to the extent that you cannot cope with it. In the first place, it is a sneaky little devil that arrives slowly over a long period of time. You can only get rid of it the same way — over a period of time.

What throws you is that suddenly you notice it, and it looks like a big, hairy monster. Your natural instincts are to fight, which you start doing without any sort of plan. You panic and that is when things get out of hand.

In the second place, you are not the **only** person who has ever had target panic and you are not the **first** to get it. Dumber people than you have had target panic and licked it because they understood that the important thing was to approach it in a positive way with a positive plan. That plan was not to condemn any one thing, but rather to work with a positive attitude toward proving that the fears were unfounded.

Fear is a natural thing. In fact, it can be a good thing. I see it as a protection for me. Webster says it is "an emotion caused by expectation of danger." Once you're convinced that there is no danger, there can be no fear — and no target panic.

A practical application of the solution for target panic

Target panic begins when you try too hard to center on the goal and remain there. You keep trying to hold still and be more perfect, more perfect, more perfect on that little spot.

No one can hold that still, and no one should try. We're human beings, not machines built to thousandths-of-an-inch tolerance with locking lugs and such.

Eventually, you get so you can't hold the pin on the gold. You have lost control.

I solved my target panic mainly through stubbornness. I wasn't going to let me beat myself.

Then **I also** took the post and dot out of the sight ring, using just the ring. That helped greatly.

For instance, if someone were to hand you a hoop two feet in diameter and tell you to look at the moon through it, you'd automatically center the hoop on the moon. If you were given a one-and-a-half inch ring and told to look at the moon through it, you would center it, too.

Now, when I have a student use the ring to conquer target panic, I first ask, "Where do you want the shot to go?"

Naturally, everyone wants it to go in the gold.

"Allright," I say, "now all you think about is where that shot is going to go. I want you, in your mind, to see that shot going in the gold."

"Ok, I see it."

"Are you sure?"

"Yes."

"Allright, now don't aim. Aiming doesn't have anything to do with it. Just keep seeing that shot go into the gold, and then go ahead and make the shot."

I have raised scores with that technique. I have a student right now with a case of "almost" target panic. He didn't have it all the time, but he did have it part of the time. He took the post and dot out and used just the ring. He hasn't had target panic since. Why? Because he's not consciously aiming. His subconscious centers that ring on the gold, and he's not trying to hold anything still. You might say that ring is helping him surround the gold and draw it into him, make it part of him and the shot . . . as opposed to attempting to assault the gold with a little dot that tries to bounce off the gold like that gold spot had a rubber barrier around it.

What we can learn from blind archers

I want to share what I have learned in several years of teaching the blind to shoot the bow and arrow for fun. I believe a message is here that might jolt the sighted shooter out of his or her complacency.

I had worked with wheelchair archers, but it had never crossed my mind that the blind could ever be archers. It's a shame that things are never done because we never think to try them. There is no way to measure what I have learned from these people about things that I (and every other griping, sighted person) should already know and be practicing.

It started when Roger Keeney, activities coordinator for the Phoenix Blind Center, asked me if I thought the blind could shoot archery and, if so, would I be interested in teaching them?

I said yes to both questions.

I limited the class to six people and the Blind Center bus transported them to the lanes the next Wednesday afternoon. Three weeks later, the center had seven more signed up and waiting for the class.

My education was about to begin.

I told them I had never worked with blind people and that I had decided to treat them no differently than I would a bunch of sighted shooters. They liked that and gave me a round of applause. So, the die was cast for the beginning of one of the nicest experiences that has happened to me in or out of coaching.

Two and a half years later, in response to a plea I made on a television newscast for someone to invent some kind of electronic sighting device for blind people, Roger Balcom of Goodyear Aerospace in Litchfield Park, Arizona, produced the sight we now use. This sight turns light into sound.

We use a spotlight on top of the butt directly above the target face. The receiver is attached to the bow with an ear plug in the ear of each archer. The highest pitch of sound is the center of the spotlight and the receiver is adjusted to put the arrow into a bulls-eye below. The field of vision (the highest pitch of sound) is about 16 inches in diameter, making it possible to aim on the light, but not necessarily dead center.

My message is that we can and should learn from their attitudes and profit from their skill in the use of those senses. The attitude of the blind toward a group of arrows, regardless of where they are on the target face, is a switch from what I am used to. (Sighted shooters get uptight about it.) When a blind person shoots an exceptional group, everyone gets excited and they all go over to the target. The general comment from the shooter is, "Now, all I have to do is move it over here in the center."

Their genuine pleasure when someone else shoots well and their spontaneous compliments to that person are rewarding to witness. The poorest shooter gets praised for a good shot by everyone in the group, including the best shooter.

If they are shooting a league, their sighted partner gets the same treatment. I have never heard a blind person condemn another for poor shooting or for anything else related to the game they are playing. No one has ever thrown a fit because their score was not as expected. They take their lumps and accept what they get, without letting everyone know that they expected more. They don't tell anyone how good they are, they never apologize for what they shoot, nor do they gripe about what they might have shot. They are not ashamed of the fruits of their honest effort.

They practice in groups, or on their own, using a target face with a small string glued on the line between each scoring ring. This makes a raised indicator so they can score their own arrows. I have silently observed a shooting match between two, three or sometimes four people and never has a shooter ever called an arrow in the high scoring ring if his fingers said it might be out.

Their approach to what they want to do, and with what they have to do it with, is refreshing. I have learned from it.

Everyone is dealt a share of life. Some seem to get more than others. But, what you get is not as important as what you do with your share. They understand that. Do you?

Mental Control   39

Is there such a thing as peaking?

How do you know that you have peaked? You never are at your utmost, are you, in shooting? None of us ever make full use of our capacity, so we're never at peak.

However, we all use it and understand it. But I feel like I'm lying when I use the word "peaking."

It doesn't mean you've gone as far as you ever can; it actually means you've gone as far as you can in your abilities at a specific time. I agree to that, but how do I know exactly where that is?

It is a useful term, though, because it signifies that you may be at or near an attainable goal as a shooter. I don't believe you should strive for perfection, because then you set a goal that will leave you frustrated, unable to build on a positive system.

I'm not going to tell a student that he/she must reach perfection. I tell them no one is perfect, but they can be closer to it than anyone else. This lets them stop trying to be perfect and helps them set a goal they think they can reach. Perfection is too far away, too hazy, too crushing when it isn't reached. You need to know that you **can** reach the goal, if you are to remain enthused and positive. You can set tough goals, but they must hold something better than a faraway promise.

The concept of peaking can work against you, and that is why I use it in only one way . . . "You're getting close" . . . "I think you're going to make it" . . . "It looks good to me" . . . "You're looking better all the time."

"I peaked too early" is a cop-out. All it says is that the shooter let down somewhere along the line. If you're worried about peaking, then you're distracted from improving your shot. You've lost sight of your goal, you're already concerned about losing. You're thinking negatively, anticipating failure.

I never tell a shooter he or she is peaked out. If they listen, and listen correctly, then I'm purposely a little dubious all the time, because they just never quite reach it. That keeps them trying, keeps them going forward.

It's a mental thing.

People of mediocre ability sometimes achieve success because they don't know enough to quit.

Bernard Baruch.

Mental Control

Chapter Three: Building the Best Form

Tailor practice programs to physical and mental needs

As any good coach knows, the key to making a student produce the best performance he or she is capable of is to analyze every aspect of the situation, both mentally and physically. He must then decide what he needs to get that performance.

The mental attitudes must be analyzed and evaluated. The desire of the student to participate in the sport is important, and ways to encourage that desire must be implemented. The determination to pursue the sport once it is started — and the understanding by the student of all the frustrations and hard work that are involved to reach a goal — have to be dealt with. The confidence of the individual in himself and the degree of his ability to learn must be judged.

A program for these mental needs must be tailored for that individual to produce the greatest amount of control with the least amount of effort.

It has been said that the mental part of shooting is not visible, but I do not agree with that assumption. It is evident and visible when a person is only half trying or is dead serious. The hardest signs to read are those which control concentration, fear of winning, fear of losing, lack of confidence — and even these become evident under the watchful eye of a good coach. The coach's ability to read the mental efforts of the student through these visible signs can be the difference that puts the shooter in the winners' circle.

The physical part of shooting is right out in front where everyone can see everything that goes on before, during and after the shot. That fact alone can produce the loss of the fine mental sharpness needed to score well.

This physical form has many faces and a reason for every one of them. I have talked about some of the physical differences confronting the coach and shooter and suggested a few instances of trading one off against the other to get a happy medium which would work to the shooter's advantage. Sometimes this is impossible, and we must live with what we have because there is no way to fix it differently or to trade for something that will relieve its severity. In that case, we take a positive attitude and produce a winner with what we have.

One physical difference worth mentioning here is what has been labeled "in line" shooting. This means that at full draw and anchor, the point of the elbow is lined up with the nock end and the point end of the arrow. The point of the elbow is then "in line" with the arrow.

This alignment is desirable; however, not many shooters have this to perfection. The ones closest to it have a distinct advantage in that any variation they may have in the release part of the shot will be less severe than those who have the same variations, but have less "in line" form.

The reason for this advantage is simple. As the arm is pulled back from the string at release, energy is applied to the arrow. When energy is applied to anything, it travels in a straight line. If both points of the arrow and the point of the elbow are lined up one with the other, as the elbow is moved back "in line," the energy will go straight down the shaft from nock to point, pushing the arrow forward in perfect harmony with the effort. If the point of the elbow is not "in line" with the other two points, the energy will be applied and travel with a slight angle from the path of the arrow.

The more the elbow is out of line, the greater the difference in the angle. Now, if you have a slight variation in your release, it stands to reason that the more "in line" the shot is, the less effect that variation will have on how the arrow travels and where it goes. If the length of the upper part of the arm is too long in relation to the length of the forearm, then the elbow cannot fold back "in line" with the arrow, because we must stop the hand at an anchor point on the face or chin before it gets there.

Changing the anchor to the side of the face will help move the elbow back more "in line"; however, there are other problems to consider if we do that. Stretching too far to achieve better "in line" form can be detrimental; however, the shooter should always extend himself **up to** that fine point of "too far."

Too much interference of the string in the chest area sometimes foils our attempt to get more in line. The positions of the head, neck, face, chin, shoulders, etc. are all factors to be reckoned wtih as the effort is made to develop a better "in line" form for the individual.

You don't have to be an "in line" shooter to shoot well, but if you can manipulate the form to some degree to accommodate it without sacrificing too much elsewhere, you can perhaps gain a few points.

A good job of mental and physical analyzing by your coach or by you of yourself if you do not have access to a good coach will produce for you a

---

Only in dictionaries does success come before work.

Best Form

great sense of confidence with the realization that everything will fall in place, producing better scores with less effort.

Not all mental and physical form is perfect. The badge of a good shooter is that he always tries to **improve** what he has now.

Practice close to the target

When you become a good shooter, you unconsciously are shooting by feel. You know how the good shot feels when you set it up, go through all your checkpoints, release it and follow through. You know what the shot will be like when it leaves the bow.

When it all works right, you undoubtedly have a mental picture of that shot in the gold before the arrow even arrives at the target, long before it arrives at the target. That's called "projecting" or "burning a hole in the gold with your eyes and mind." Top shooters feel that they are mentally willing that arrow into the gold.

One of the best ways to develop the feel of the shot is to stand close to a target butt, without a target face, and shoot shot after shot with your eyes closed. Many times I have had a student with a fault in form or in rhythm and had them cure it when they used this practice technique. Shooting at an empty butt with their eyes closed, their mind's eye concentrated solely on the feel of the shot.

You have to know that. You have to compliment yourself when the shot feels good. It reinforces all kinds of positive images in your conscious and subconscious minds, and in your muscle memory.

The ones that are terrible, all you know is that they felt terrible. You don't try to fix them, just try to do better on the next shot.

You need to have your eyes shut because with them open you tend to aim. You want to know where the shot went. And when you shoot, your concentration does not remain on the feel of the shot.

You haven't trained your subconscious yet to understand the feel of the well-put-together shot. So, in shooting with your eyes shut, you're consciously feeling it, developing that feel. If you're consciously feeling it, then every time you do it right you are telling your subconscious "I like that." Every time you shoot and it doesn't feel right, you tell your subconscious almost without knowing it "That didn't feel good. I want it better." So you dismiss that feel and concentrate on doing it better with the next shot.

I had a student once with a release problem he couldn't break. He was a 14 year old kid, crazy about shooting. He practiced seven hours a day. He wanted to be good, so he kept on practicing, thinking that the more he practiced the better he would become.

I couldn't get him to break the bad habit, and suddenly it dawned on me that the reason he couldn't stop it was that he was practicing it so much.

I asked his mother if she would support me if I took him off shooting and she said she would.

His lessons were on Monday. He shot JOAD (Junior Olympic Archery Development program) on Saturday morning. So that Monday after his lesson I said, "Give your mother your bow. Don't pick it up until you come to JOAD Saturday morning. Just stay away from shooting a while."

I thought he was going to cry.

"Can't I practice?"

"No. I don't want you to practice. Not one shot. And when you get to JOAD Saturday, shoot your six practice arrows and **stop.** Then shoot your arrows for score, put your bow in its case and go home. Come back Monday for your regular lesson, but don't touch the bow until you get here. No Sunday practicing," I said.

When he returned Saturday for JOAD shooting, I purposely avoided him. I didn't ask his mother how he was, and I made it difficult for him to talk to me.

The following Monday, when he came in for his lesson, I asked, "How did you do at JOAD Saturday?"

"I shot my highest score ever," he said. He sounded surprised.

I didn't make much of it. "That's nice; that's good," was about all I said.

After that lesson I told him, "You can shoot for 20 minutes Wednesday evening, but stand up close to an empty butt and shoot with your eyes shut." I'll bet he thought I'd gone right off the deep end.

"But can't I practice more than that?"

Now that he'd shot his highest score ever, he wanted to practice even more so he could improve upon it.

"Nope," I said. "Twenty minutes Wednesday, then nothing until you shoot JOAD Saturday morning."

He cured that release problem without me, and it didn't take long.

His problem was that just as he began his release, he'd lose a bit of back tension. His drawing elbow would slide forward a little bit, then his sub-conscious would take over, pull it back and release. With his mind on aiming, he couldn't feel it. But in the dark, with his entire concentration on the feel of the shot, he picked it up in a hurry.

I believe any archer would be well advised to do this now and then during his regular schedule. Just go back and groove that feel again. You can pick up right away on the rhythm and the feel. You'll end up making the right, grooved feel even more deeply implanted in your subconscious and your muscle memory.

Any time an archer starts having a bit of trouble, I always ask, "Have you practiced any recently with your eyes shut?"

A lot of them haven't, simply because they want to shoot arrows so much they can't bear the thought of taking their concentration off them and onto building a shot which will ultimately give them better results when they **do** shoot for score.

The only reason for shooting close to a target butt is, of course, so you don't lose arrows. I think everyone understands that.

Many shooters are surprised at the tightness of the groups they shoot with their eyes shut. They discover that if they just relax and put the shot together, the results often seem to take care of themselves.

The best helping hands are at the ends of your own arms.

Precise anchors produce better scores

It is most important that the hand which holds the string and the nock end of the arrow at full draw be anchored in a precise manner somewhere about the face. This anchor and its placement is very important to consistent form and better scores at the target butt.

There are various anchors for different kinds of archery games, which are dictated by what you are trying to do in that game. Bowhunters use a high, fast anchor to take care of that split second of time they have to get an arrow off, while the target shooter uses a low anchor generally to lower the rear of the arrow so he can get longer distances with a lighter bow.

The most common target anchor is under the chin, with the string touching the center of the chin and nose. These two string contacts are reference points which will make the shot more consistent. The head must be tilted sideways so a right-handed shooter is looking on the left side of the string, above and in line with the arrow.

However, because everyone varies physically, it is virtually impossible to make everyone use this anchor with success. If the archer has a short neck, short nose, jutting jaw or any wrong combination of such things, he is carrying a handicap which could be eliminated to some degree with a modification of this anchor.

There is absolutely nothing wrong with this type of anchor for those who can use it, and I have no quarrel with it if they can. However, I do quarrel with those shooters who are so narrow-minded they cannot accept a different or modified version when the shooter's natural physical build demands it. No one needs to be saddled with something that does not fit him.

There is also another anchor, generally referred to as "side-of-face." Some of our best archers use this one or some modification of it.

Charlie Sandlin of Flagstaff, Arizona, won the world championship in Finland in 1963 using a complete side-of-face anchor.

● Joan McDonald, a top Canadian archer, demonstrating a thought on anchoring. Finding the right anchor which suits you and your physical structure is critical. Use an anchor which: 1) Feels comfortable; 2) is easily duplicated, shot to shot; 3) fits your individual form. You'll need to experiment a bit, and when you do so, be certain you give each experiment a fair trial.

A complete side-of-face anchor would be to turn the head in a natural position as you look at the target and pull the string to the side of the chin until the string touches the corner of the mouth. The tip of the first finger will be anchored under the jawbone. (A ledge tab is a great asset for most anchors and especially this one.) In this position, the head is now turned enough so the string will not hit the nose upon release.

The shooter's head is in a nicely balanced, natural position, looking straight ahead through the center of his glasses (if he wears them) and not the extreme corner past his nose. He is looking above and directly in line with the arrow and on the left side of the string (right-hand shooter) without screwing the head into an unnatural position. Everything feels natural because it is, and it takes no contortions to produce it.

Most shooters using the center-of-chin-and-nose anchor have to pull the chin toward the body at full draw. This is caused by the fact that the nose is just not long enough to reach the string without tucking the chin. (If they must tuck the chin, a change to the side-of-face anchor should **not** increase their draw length.) If the chin is **not** tucked in, the draw will be increased to some extent when the switch is made to side-of-face anchor, which also puts the elbow more in line with the arrow.

The follow-through of the drawing arm after the explosion of the shot seems to bug a lot of people as well. I don't think it should.

The follow-through is controlled by back tension. When the string hand completely relaxes, and the release of the string occurs, the follow-through is a graceful movement — if the form has been set up to explode correctly. As you hold the elbow back to keep the bow at full draw you have stopped and are holding at or on your anchor point. But the muscles

Best Form

holding that elbow back should be alive and constantly pulling like a spring being stretched and held there.

When the back of the hand that holds the string relaxes, the spring-loaded arm will pull the elbow backward in a smooth follow-through that is effortless and consistent. Care should be used in keeping the elbow as level as possible in its backward motion. The hand and forearm should not be raised above the line of the arrow. Avoid the natural inclination to torque the string hand from its unnatural vertical position on the string to the natural horizontal position after the explosion.

The tips of the fingers should be touching the neck and the back of the hand should be vertical at the conclusion of the follow-through to ensure a clean, consistent release and higher scores on the target.

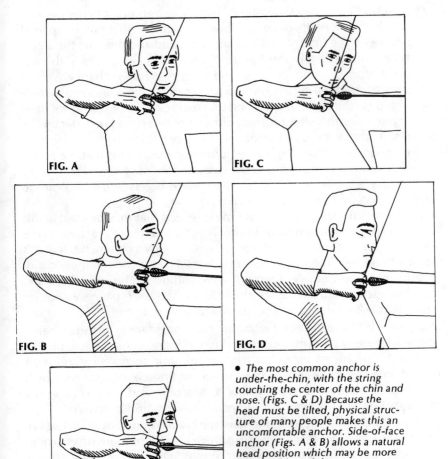

FIG. A

FIG. C

FIG. B

FIG. D

FIG. E

● *The most common anchor is under-the-chin, with the string touching the center of the chin and nose. (Figs. C & D) Because the head must be tilted, physical structure of many people makes this an uncomfortable anchor. Side-of-face anchor (Figs. A & B) allows a natural head position which may be more comfortable and thus more successful. Fig. E shows a high (corner of the mouth) and fast anchor bowhunters prefer and is suitable with heavy draw weight bows.*

47

The all-important bow arm unit

Many, many times in my 35 years of coaching competitive archers I have been asked what one thing in style or method, what one phase of the shooting form, is the most important to a competitive shooter. I have an idea that most coaches, and shooters, have some one thing they feel is very important to them for good, consistent grouping, one single, necessary thing that is over and above all the rest in importance.

Perhaps it is debatable that any one thing is more important than any other one, but I think it is and I teach this idea to my students. I must point out here, however, as I do in answering questions personally or in teaching students, that it takes a heap of things all put together in balance, and controlled to the "Nth" degree, to consistently shoot top scores.

I think my "most important thing" will make a good shot even better. I believe that what happens to the "bow arm unit" in that precise span of time between the instant of the brain command and the time the arrow clears the bowstring is the key to a successful shot. This is the last ingredient added to the recipe for good scores. Whatever happens at the exact instant that our brain gives the string fingers the command to relax their hold on the string is the thing that makes everything else we have put together for that shot produce either the results we are expecting or the results that we did not want.

The tragic thing about this often unrecognized fact is that the coach cannot really see it happen, and the student does not exactly feel it or for that matter even believe it. Buddy, it's there big as life, and it can be proven.

Any reference to a measure of time or speed that may be used in this article is for comparison only. I think I read somewhere that it takes the brain 70 milli-seconds to give any part of our body a command. If that is so, the brain has time to give us more than 14 commands in one second. It probably does, too, since we can stand without falling, breathe, walk, talk, smile, close our eyes and unlock the car at the same time. A shooter can use this knowledge to his advantage.

Let's say we have a shooter who has a burning desire to be top archer in the world. He is determined to do this and believes he can. He understands the problems he must face, has the time to practice and is an experienced tournament shooter. He has the finest of equipment which is tuned to perfection. He is young and strong, and his form appears flawless. Yet he is "always a bridesmaid, never a bride." Why?

It could be that at the exact moment the brain commands the release of the string fingers, a small movement (even the tightening of an arm or shoulder muscle from unnecessary tension) in his bow arm unit, for any reason whatsoever, louses up his shot. If **any** part of this bow arm unit moves only one thirty-second of an inch, before the impact of the explosion hits the shooter, it can put the arrow somewhere other than dead center. This error of movement is also magnified because the unit continues moving all through the explosion, like a shotgun moves when shooting a bird in flight. It is a small amount and it will vary for many reasons depending on what caused it.

When the brain gives the command for the fingers to relax, every part of the body knows that command has been given and that this is the beginning of the end of the effort. In my opinion **this** is the most important moment. As an example, at the instant the command is given, the shoulder could slightly quit holding its position because it anticipates that the shot will soon be over. The elbow could anticipate the finish and not stay rigid. The wrist could do the same thing.

The bow arm must hold the physical weight of the six-pound bow after the explosion so it could begin to get ready at the instant of command, without waiting for the weight to manifest itself. The entire arm unit could decide that the show is over at the moment the command is given to the fingers to release, and begin to relax because its work is soon over. The concentration of aiming could also start to give up and quit working too soon. And on and on.

The colors of the school of experience are black and blue.

Now I ask you, what other single thing in the whole scheme of shooting technique is so dependent upon so many other things to make it work? I can think of nothing that has so many operations dictating the success or failure of the shot as does the one-thousandth of a second of time between the brain command and the fingers actually leaving the bowstring. I think this is the most important instant of all. This is the time in which you **must** exercise the control necessary to hold still until the shock of explosion hits.

Oh, yes, I agree with you, 100 percent control is all you need. That would solve everything. However, unless you know what the problem is and understand its importance, you don't generally control down to the fine points that we are talking about.

International coach, and my good friend, Len Cardinale takes care of how best to achieve the kind of control needed for a perfect shot in his explanation of follow through. He says, and I quote, "Follow through is the continuation of your form as it was before the explosion." Unquote.

Think that through very thoroughly and shoot better. It is the answer to what I consider to be the one most important thing for a competitive archer to master.

Discouragement is the illegitimate child of false expectations.
Lloyd Ogilvie

Prepare your shot right to avoid flinches

At almost any tournament you can hear someone say, "I really blew it when I flinched that arrow."

Ninety-five percent of the time, that's about as far as that shooter will go concerning why he really blew it. To him, he just blew it. No reason, he just flinched and that's it.

We all know there is a reason for everything, no matter how large or how small it may be. I think it behooves all of us to do a little reflecting about any shot we flinch on.

Physically-induced flinches are those which could be caused by someone touching you while you're at full draw, or by a noisy truck passing or a big disturbance behind you. All of these can make you lose control. They are conditions that are generally easy to see and because of that they seem to be the most common cause to the shooter.

Such situations demand a great amount of control. I might add here that if you do not practice keeping control under those circumstances, then you will forever have trouble.

Mentally-induced flinches are those sneaky little devils that come in all sizes and at any time. Some seem so innocent, we would never think to accuse them of being there.

These are the flinches I am most concerned about. They are often so small the coach can barely see them, and the shooter is not aware of them.

I drill into every one of my students that a flinch is caused by an indecision because their shot preparation was not accepted 100 percent by their subconscious self. This is the one part of themselves that, through habit, they have taught **exactly** what they want it to **accept** and what they want it to **reject.**

When there is a rejection, the message to the brain saying "hold everything" comes too late to stop the explosion. The later these rejections occur, the smaller the visible signs are that they did occur. Some signs, as I have said before, are so small that we wonder what happened.

What happens here is that we are trying to do two things at once. We are trying to let the explosion do its thing and at the **very same instance** we decide to prevent it.

To keep a flinch from occurring, we must assemble a lot of things to make a shot perfect. Some of these things are large and obvious.

Some of the most important ones are invisible, such as control and concentration.

I believe we tend to worry about the more obvious things and get very careless in our efforts where the not-so-obvious and the invisible ones are concerned. We might say, then, that concentration is the key to the elimination of flinches.

Best Form

Could we say here that the loss of control caused by a loud noise, a poke in the ribs or a disturbance behind the shooter could have been prevented had the shot been 100 percent prepared? I think we could. Being 100 percent prepared includes 100 percent concentration. Had the shooter been trained under those circumstances, there would have been no flinch.

A flinch is not a bad thing, really. It is your little helper. In its true sense, it is nothing more than an indicator that tells you to shape up your form, that you are getting careless. If you like, you can also feel good because it is saying your subconscious apparatus still functions.

Don't give yourself the devil when you flinch. Put that cussin' energy to a better use. **Prepare** the shot so there will be no rejection of any part of it.

Remember:
Complete preparation of the shot comes first.
The explosion comes next.
Then the follow-through, which makes it all tie together as one in a gracefully executed shot.

Don't be so busy cutting wood that you don't have time to sharpen your axe.

Control your breathing and pick up points

Swimmers, runners and competitive gun shooters control their breathing for better performance in their sports. Even an artist painting a delicate line on a portrait holds his breath to control movement.

A common complaint by archers in regard to breathing while shooting is that they have tried to regulate it, but "it doesn't work." They can hold the sight pin steady for a short period of time, but it starts to wiggle before they get the shot off.

No one can hold the sight absolutely still. With the arm extended and under the pressure of the draw, your sight pin will move on every beat of your heart — not much, but it will move. This should come as no surprise to anyone, since the arm is not supported in any way. The real trick is to learn to eliminate as much movement as possible and then compensate for whatever movement is left.

Too many shooters think that anyone who shoots well can hold the sight pin steadily on the gold for an indefinite period of time. They then destroy a good shot by trying to find the steadiness nobody has.

Their confidence suffers when they discover it is impossible for them to do what they think others can do. Then they give up on the project and, somewhere down the line, become unaware of exactly where the sight pin is when the shot explodes.

Trying to hold the sight pin that steadily only creates heavy tension in the bow arm that, in turn, produces more movement than they had before. The more they force the issue, the more frustrated they become.

Understanding these problems will help the archer relax bow arm tension and obtain better control for a steadier shooting unit.

The breathing problem is different with different shooters, but by trial and error a system can emerge which will help an individual archer control it.

Controlled breathing will definitely steady the sight to almost absolute stillness, providing the bow arm is not tied up in a tense struggle to force it still. You must find a breathing routine that will produce the greatest amount of steadiness, and train yourself to get rid of the arrow during the time period in which you can maintain control. For those who have the habit of holding a long time in an attempt to get steadier, getting something done in a newly-set time period will be rough.

I have established a breathing routine that has met with success among my students. As they prepare the arrow for the string, they take a deep breath. They let it all out as they raise the bow, take another breath, draw and anchor. As the pin begins to settle on the bullseye, they slowly let their breath half out and hold it. By this time the pin should be settled in the gold, and they should have no trouble holding the breath for four or five seconds. If the shot set-up has been properly prepared and their breathing synchronized with it, four or five seconds should be more than enough time to shoot a perfect shot.

As I said, different archers will require different methods to control breathing and movement. The exact method is not important, as long as the results provide a smooth pattern and higher scores.

When aiming isn't really aiming

Sometimes the most commonplace thing is also a most important thing. It may be so common you think you know all about how to do it, and you tell yourself you always do it. Well, I have found that sometimes — in fact, a great many times — what you think you do, you sure as heck **do not** do, which makes it sort of double trouble. If you weren't even concerned about it, that would be a neutral base. But since you're doing the opposite of what you think you're doing, that makes it a double move in the wrong direction.

Aiming is a good example of this. Too many shooters do not know **how** to aim. The expert shooters, as well as the mediocre ones, can and do have this trouble, knowingly or unknowingly.

Everybody thinks they know how to aim . . . I don't agree they do.

This aiming "problem" is also next to impossible for the coach to prove sometimes. It can be and is done to some degree, but it takes a lot of analyzing, gut feeling and accusation on the part of the coach to ferret it out. Even then, you would be hard pressed at first to convince the student that he or she was not really aiming, for seldom do they know that they are not aiming in the sense that we are talking here.

There are 50 different types or degrees of aiming, but I shall talk about that down-to-earth, super fine, absolute degree you must have to shoot the scores you dream about. (You know that dreams generally come true in direct proportion to the degree of effort we exercise toward that end.)

In the first place, you never aim until you have every other part of your form put together for the shot. The last thing you do before the shot is aim. I've observed that a majority of shooters pull up, put the pin somewhere on the target and then as soon as the pin indicates it is on or close to the gold they "let 'er go."

Many, many times, I have asked, "Were you really ready for the shot?" They have answered, "Yeah, the pin was on."

Yet I could easily see their form was not prepared for the shot. They let it go because they had never really understood that **aiming is only part of a good shot** and it is to be done only after every other part of the shot form is put together.

Just putting the sight pin on the 10 ring is not aiming. Concentration on holding it there after every part of the form is prepared is aiming. Think about this and try it sometime — we **anchor** the drawing hand at the chin, we put the sight pin in the 10 ring and that **anchors** the bow hand. If everything else is prepared correctly, we are now **ready to aim.**

Aiming is now the amount of concentration you put in to melt that sight pin into the gold and burn a hole through that 10 ring for the arrow to enter. That, my friends, is aiming. That is concentration. That is a 10.

Let's run this whole shot sequence through so we might better understand one another. Putting the shot together means settling into a known feeling that everything is in the right place and that you feel and know you are now (regardless of where the sight pin is) ready to aim, which is 100 percent pure concentration. The shot explodes and you must not falter one iota in your concentration on aiming until the arrow has arrived in the 10 ring (which is pure concentrated follow-through). Then, and only then, may you become aware that the world is still around you.

Too many people think and feel that they do all of these things, but their scores tell us they don't. In reality, they quit too soon on each one.

If everyone would put the shot together 100 percent (which is getting that feeling), aim (which is pure concentration) and follow through (which is continued concentration), there would be an abundance of Paces, McKinneys and Ryons, because that's how they do it.

Aiming — your second anchor point

Question: The eye controls an archer's aiming in what way?

Answer: By anchoring the sight pin on the 10 ring.

The key word is anchor. I like to think and teach that putting the sight pin on the 10 ring is not aiming in the same sense that we think of it in everyday life. In archery, this so-called aiming is only another anchor point.

We have two anchor points to put into effect when we prepare the shot — 1) under the chin or side of mouth, which is controlled by feel, and 2) sight pin which is controlled by visual perception.

Aiming is then done by concentrating on and believing that the arrow will arrive at the same spot on the target face where you have that little pin anchored.

Concentration must be absolute at this point. It must go hand in hand with believing that the arrow will arrive where it is intended to go.

"Believing" is another key word.

When we put the pin on the 10 ring, the pin should be thought of as being just another part of our physical form. It would be like anchoring the hand and the string on the face. You would simply anchor the pin on the 10 and then control that anchor the same way you would control the string alignment on the bow. Your eye could then tell you when it was on and when it was off the target's center.

It would then become another part of the form that is delegated to the subconscious mind, to be executed correctly while you concentrate and believe that the arrow will hit where you have the sight pin anchored.

At this point, through concentration, you think that you're going to place an arrow where you have the sight pin anchored. You aren't concentrating on just trying to hold a sight pin on the spot and having it disappear when the explosion occurs. You aren't concentrating on the shot because it's in the bow; you're concentrating on where you expect the arrow to hit.

I have continued to use the word aim as we use it in everyday life, but I am only trying to convey a thought that suggests we must go further and dig deeper into this important mental preparation of our form. We should learn how to manipulate the shot to the spot on the face where we want it to go by channelling our concentration in the right direction at the right time and for the right reason.

I am not condemning anyone for aiming as they do now. I am suggesting they change their conscious concentration efforts from just holding a pin on a spot to concentrating on the spot they want the shot to go and believing it will arrive there.

To explore another angle, a good reason for this type of thinking is that when we're concentrating on just holding the sight pin steady on the spot and the explosion happens, the sight pin disappears from our vision and the concentration we had on holding the pin is gone as well.

This brings up the concept of aiming through the shot, which most everyone agrees is essential to good scores. Aiming through the shot means holding your concentration on what you are doing until the arrow hits the target. It would be very hard to concentrate on something that isn't there anymore. If that is true, then we must change our goal; it would be next to impossible to aim through if we had lost what we were aiming with.

I repeat, we should anchor the sight pin where we want it, delegate its performance to the subconscious mind, and then concentrate on where we want the shot to hit. It matters not what the explosion of the shot does to that anchor point. It **does** matter what we are concentrating on when the explosion happens.

Learn to concentrate on what you want to happen. Learn to know when you are not concentrating.

A steady elbow helps build better back tension

I do not belabor a shooter with a lot of "do this or that" because of my belief that I can get him to use back muscles, as I want them to be used, without confusing him with a lot of scientific explanations.

I am not against scientific explanations. Scientific information is important if properly used. It is encouraging to know that through the efforts being done in sports medicine for most sports, archers are learning and advancing into a new era. However, I believe we sometimes get our explanations more complicated than we need to, and that can cause more harm than good.

My reluctance to explain too much about back tension to the rank and file of my students is caused by the fact that far too many have been confused by someone who insists that it must be done but can't tell them how to do it.

When that student is confused, he has no idea how to pick out a certain muscle or group of muscles and make them work. The harder he tries, the more likely he is to arrive at a solution that can louse up some part of an otherwise perfect form.

When I get someone who is confused in this area, I tell him we will forget the back and work on it later. This is supposed to relieve the student's anxiety on that problem.

I will later transfer the pull to the back muscles without telling him how to do it. In fact, I do not tell him when he begins to pull those muscles correctly. That comes later or never, whichever is better for the student.

All I ask of a student, or anyone else for that matter, is that he be sure the **elbow** of his drawing arm is being held back in position without creeping forward. (The key word is elbow.)

I want the student to **think** and **hold** the **elbow** back. I don't want him to think and pull with the back muscles, and I don't want him to think and pull the arrow out from under the clicker.

As the elbow habit is perfected, the student is relieved of the confusion, and the natural use of the muscles will be the results. This allows the shooter to concentrate on other areas.

There are **two things** that must work in conjunction with this concept and be a part of the habit. (I have never had any problem in this area.)

1) The shooter must learn how to relax the forearm, and not use its muscles to pull and hold.

2) The arm from elbow to shoulder should also be as relaxed as possible, and although those muscles help hold the elbow back, it should not be a deliberate or conscious effort.

Relaxing as much as possible will let the proper arm muscles help the back do what it is supposed to do. When these things are accomplished, the back muscles work to hold the elbow back.

For the less confused who are ready to learn how the back muscles really work but can't feel them do it, there is a way to show them that feeling. Open the shooter's stance to about a 45-degree angle, stand behind him and hold his hips in that position to prevent twisting as he draws. Then have him draw, aim and shoot.

If he can't pull to full draw, adjust the stance a little bit so he can reach full draw.

After he gets that feel in the back, modify the stance back to where it will work best for that shooter. You could discover that a more open stance will help that particular student improve his pull, hold and release.

Once the shooter has been made aware of his technique and the improvement it makes on his scores, he will never want to go back to the old stance. It won't feel right anymore.

The best bow hand position

Placing the hand on the bow handle in a comfortable position **may not** be the ideal way for you to shoot the consistent shots necessary to produce the good groups essential for good scores. This **does not mean** that a good hand position has to be uncomfortable.

There is an optimum position for **you** that will produce the least torque (right or left) on your bow handle. This optimum position will also take less effort to consistently control the wrist of your bow arm.

Generally, the reason a change in your hand position on the bow feels uncomfortable is simply because you are used to the old way. Any

Best Form

deviation from that familiar position telegraphs to you the fact that it has been moved. Your urge is to "correct" it. That is a natural response.

However, after a diligent effort to practice the new position, it will begin to feel comfortable and the better groups will soon convince you that you made a good move. Many times I have moved a student's hand position only one-sixteenth of an inch and reduced his/her group to as much as one-half the original size.

The size and shape of your hand, and the size and shape of the grip on the bow handle, will tell you to some extent where your personal hand position should be.

There are two lines of pressure on the bow handle back toward the shooter at full draw. Those two lines will dictate how sensitive your situation is. One line goes up to the bone of the bow arm; the other is the direction the string follows to the anchor point. If the position of the hand on the bow does not balance these two lines, torque will result.

Since we can't draw the string directly up the bow arm and thus have all pressure in one line — which would mean there would be no torque — we must draw up the side of the arm to the chin and then adjust the hand position to balance the two lines of pressure. These two lines form an angle. The degree of that angle will also dictate where your hand position should be on the bow.

For some shooters, a small move of the hand can bring dramatic results. For others, satisfactory results will come only after a good amount of trial.

The position I find which works best for most people is neither complicated nor hard to maintain. Simply put, it is placing the hand on the bow grip so the line down the center of the arm runs into the center of the bow. The pressure on the bow handle is then closer to being equal to the pressure of the line the drawn string follows.

These two lines of pressure form a vee. The arm line can be adjusted left or right to eliminate torque by moving your bow hand. Remember, too, that not every bow hand can eliminate all torque.

People who shoot with a straight wrist have the right idea, but I believe 99 percent of them can't master that style because wrists are just not strong enough to have the consistency needed for the job.

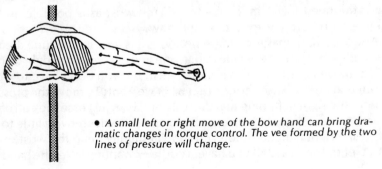

● *A small left or right move of the bow hand can bring dramatic changes in torque control. The vee formed by the two lines of pressure will change.*

To find your hand position, hold your bow arm out toward the target (without the bow), fingers straight out and the hand held perpendicular. Turn your hand clockwise one-eighth turn. (One-quarter turn would have the hand horizontal.) Hold the arm, wrist and hand in that position.

Relax the wrist and let it bend.

Draw the knuckles up and toward you without moving the arm. Have someone put the bow in your hand and without moving the position of the hand close your fingers gently around the bow. If you are correct, the little finger may not even touch the bow.

The "life line" in the palm of your hand is now important to you as you adjust your hand on the grip. The base of the thumb is separated from the heel of the hand by the life line. Place the "corner" of the grip on the life line. (The "corner" would be the line where the face of the grip would meet the left side of the grip (for a right handed shooter).) If executed correctly, the line up the bone of the bow arm will be running into the center of the bow.

The wrist is to be relaxed backward completely, with the bow resting completely on the base of the thumb. The wrist must be controlled right or leftward. However, the whole point of positioning the hand is to take

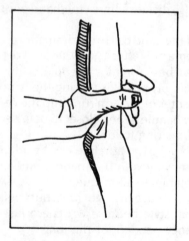

• The whole point of positioning the hand is to take away the need for as much control of the wrist as is possible and, of course, to relieve torque on the bow. In most instances, this means a low wrist position.

away the need for as much control of the wrist as is possible and, of course, to relieve the torque on the bow.

After you have mastered these positions it is time to fine tune them so you will be as close as possible to that fine line of zero left or right torque.

The movement to do this is in the wrist, but you don't have to worry about that. We will use a trick to get what we want: To move the pressure over to the right in finding that "no torque" line, just ease the end of the thumb toward the target. Let the hand and knuckles move a little to the left (for a right handed shooter). That will slightly bend the wrist — but don't let the arm twist. If you have trouble — wanting to let the hand slip back toward the right at the wrist because the position is new or because the hand is sweaty — just think "I will put a little pressure on the thumb, like pushing it toward the target." That should hold it there but not move it. When the thinking process becomes a habit, you will control the whole unit with ease.

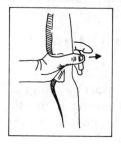

● If your hand wants to slip back toward the right (right handed shooter), just tell yourself "I will put a little pressure on the thumb, like pushing toward the target." That should hold it there but not move it.

Eliminating as much torque as is possible with a hand position that fits **you,** leaving the bow hand completely relaxed (including the fingers), will let the arrow clear the bow without interference from you. In that relaxed state, the hand will fall forward as the bow jumps forward on the explosion. The sling, not the fingers, will catch the bow. Only when the bow hits the sling do the fingers curl around the bow for positive control.

When the torque on the handle is eliminated, the string travels in a straighter line. This helps those who have very little clearance on the bow arm.

One other thing that can cause the bow and string to torque to the left toward the arm (right handed shooter), is the release of the string. If that release is not executed by a complete, spontaneous relaxing of the string fingers, you will still have some torque to the left to eliminate.

What I have shared with you here is not a cure-all for torque, but it should help.

Low wrist style best

I believe archers are better off with a low wrist style. The high wrist, or straight wrist, would be the most perfect grip position anyone could have, but very few people can shoot a high wrist for an extended period of time and do well with it. Very few people . . . only those with big, strong wrists . . . can shoot a straight wrist through a tournament without torquing the bow. It's worse at the end than at the start, usually because the wrist tires from all that pressure against it.

When you can relax the hand completely, let it rise up so the base of the thumb is against the handle as a low wrist, then keep that position, full draw pressure is against bone and not against muscle.

This gives you a positive base to work from instead of a negative one.

Knowing that a straight wrist may tire is a negative influence on your concentration and performance.

To catch lions, you must think in terms of lions, not mice.
Thomas Drier

Creeping, collapsing and the differences

There's confusion among archers on the exact meanings of "creeping" and "collapsing." Some believe that creeping is the slight forward movement of the arrow while you're supposedly holding still at full draw and aiming. Others call that collapsing.

Creeping and collapsing are two separate problems, but they both deal with physical form.

Creeping is when your elbow is moving to your right (right handed shooter) and coming forward. Your anchor slips forward, too.

Collapsing is when you stand at full draw, your anchor holds solid but you begin to twist the body and bend the bow arm at the shoulder. You're hinged at the shoulder, and you sort of fold together like closing two halves of a book.

Making sure that you and your coach know what the other means when you talk of these problems is the first step in correcting them. When I have a student with a collapsing problem, I simply tell them they're collapsing and tell them to straighten up. I'll tell them a lot of things along with that to hit them with the problem, to make them pay attention to what I say. Then I'll suddenly click my heels together, salute like a soldier and say "Yes, sir." That may be a bit comic, but it works. The student gets the point and, unless he or she is a chronic case, the problem stops.

I also tell students to watch the point of their arrow, watch it until they **know** they're creeping. I have to do this, because often neither their subconscious nor their conscious will believe me.

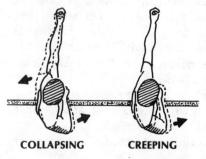

● When you creep, your drawing elbow and hand move forward. When you collapse, your bow shoulder moves back, your drawing arm and shoulder move forward and you tend to bend like an open book being closed. Confusion on these points can slow down your solving of them.

COLLAPSING   **CREEPING**

Best Form

I just say, "Ok, as long as you don't believe me, just pull it back and hold it."

They'll pull the arrow back and hold it and then watch it move forward as if it had a mind of its own. Yet they'll swear they're pulling as hard as they can.

Another technique which works well to conquer creeping and collapsing is to pull the arrow completely back off the rest until it falls on the shelf. I have students do this because I want their muscles to get past the locking position . . . and, yes, you **do** lock your muscles. They're not allowed to let down; they must pull through the clicker and off the back of the arrow rest. This eliminates the barrier of the automatic stop.

The trouble with our idea of success is that we too often measure where we are and not how far we have come.

Peek — a boo boo

Everyone knows what peeking is, but 98 percent of all shooters don't know why they peek, don't know when they peek. And some don't believe it when they do peek.

The reason anyone peeks is because he puts a higher priority on wanting to know where the arrow landed, or watching the arrow come in, rather than wanting it in the gold. Eventually that switching of priorities will bite you.

If you start a little mistake, one that won't hurt you a bit right now, that's sowing a bad seed. That's also why I coach defensively. I will stop a little something I see developing, nip it in the bud.

Peeking is a **lack of concentration and follow through.** You shove the bow aside or move your hand so you can see the arrow when, instead, you should be mentally burning a hole in the gold, a hole which your

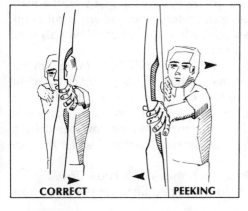

● When you peek, you move the bow to the right and the head to the left (right handed shooter), instead of letting the bow move to the left slightly like it should and holding the head still.

CORRECT   PEEKING

arrow will disappear into. Eventually, head movement will create body movement, and then you're a mess.

Many expert peekers will release, peek, then follow through in such a manner that they refuse to believe they ever peeked.

I learned from some sports medicine specialists that it takes only 70 milliseconds for your brain to give a command to your muscles, and it takes another 70 milliseconds for your muscles to react to that command. So in 1.4 tenths of a second that shot is on its way. In that time, you can make up your mind to see where the arrow goes. Expert peekers can pick up the arrow two-thirds of the way to the target. That's a fast peek!

Also, in the 70 milliseconds it takes your muscles to release the string, you can lose concentration. When that happens, you've lost it all, but you really don't think so.

That problem is correctable, though. I've done it often with students. Just getting them to concentrate through that 70 milliseconds helps them shoot better.

The problem encountered down the line with body movement means that you could well be beginning to peek as you release, while the arrow is still being influenced by the string. It may not be much, but any undue influence is too much. The only reason anyone stands there to hold a follow through is so they will hold still during those 140 milliseconds of command and release.

Elbow "tricks" can solve clicker problems

A high school archery coach once asked me if I had any tricks she could use to make her students understand how to pull with the muscles of the back as they were attempting to make the arrow pull through the clicker. She was having all kinds of trouble and getting nowhere. Her question was not one she really expected an answer to, but was sort of a joke, voiced out of frustrations we sometimes feel when we are at wit's end.

Her expression was one of surprise when I told her I definitely used "tricks" to assist in the making of a champion.

In regard to the question above, the trick would be to make him pull the correct back muscles without making him dig back in memory for the name and position of the muscle or group of muscles he should use to pull the arrow point from under the clicker. Not many coaches can name the muscles or their exact positions or even explain just how to pull them. Most students can't either, and they become confused when they are told to just **pull** with the back.

The trick is to make them do it when they don't know how.

To understand why it is so hard for some people to get the arrow from under the clicker requires a bit of understanding as to what that particular person may think he is trying to do. You might possibly say, "Well, dummy, he's trying to pull it out so it will click," and you would be right. However, through conscious or unconscious thought, he's wondering where the point is, how much farther it needs to go, and since he is pulling his best why it doesn't click. The harder he thinks he pulls, the more **all** his muscles tense — and if it happens to click, the arrow will never be where he wants it to be. If it won't click he lets down and tries again, perhaps with the same results.

Unless the yellow flag comes up, telling him that he has only 30 seconds to complete his shooting. He can then shoot two arrows in 20 seconds or less. They may not be where he wanted them, but they will be close, and he'll probably be able to pull the arrow from under the clicker with no trouble.

Why? Through deliberate thought or unconscious thought, he has now changed his **priority.** He is no longer wondering where the point of the arrow is under the clicker. He no longer wonders why it doesn't click. He doesn't even think how he could pull it out. His priority now is to beat the clock. He already knew how to make the clicker click. All he needed was something to take his mind off where the point of the arrow was, how close it was to clicking or what muscles he used to make it click.

So how do we arrive at that perfect or near-perfect execution of clicking the clicker without the use of the yellow flag? I think it is simple and very easy. Some will agree, some won't. Some will give it an honest effort, others will only play with it.

If you have your form as good as it should be, you will be pulling the arrow point consistently to some exact length or place on the bow. That being the case, you will set your clicker so that only one-eighth or three-sixteenths inch of the point is under the clicker at full draw, waiting to be pulled out. One-eighth is perfect; one-quarter inch is unnecessary.

Please note that the question at the beginning was: How do you get people to understand how to use the correct back muscles to pull the arrow from under the clicker?

Here is the trick. At full draw, the forearm, elbow, upper arm and shoulder of the drawing unit should be in the semi-relaxed state (not really pulling). The fingers are hooked on the string in the first joint, and the hand (at the wrist) is relaxed and in line. You have aimed and you need to hear a click to proceed with the shot. At this point, teach yourself to move the elbow back toward the shooter behind you.

That is all you think about or try to do. Practice that thought process until it becomes automatic and is an unconscious working part of the shot.

At this point you have done two important things. You used the correct back muscles, and, without effort, you made the clicker click. You have now made the backward movement of the elbow your **new priority.** When you are ready for the explosion you do not know or care where the point of the arrow is. That is irrelevant and not your priority at this point. If you have trouble doing this simple maneuver, it will indicate that your priority is slipping.

Another thing which gets a shooter in trouble with the clicker is the fact that he'll try to be really careful because he's afraid the sight will move off the gold if he doesn't pull slowly. This produces a stop-go-stop-go movement that eventually makes the archer think he has pulled further back than he actually has.

There is nothing wrong with being careful or pulling slowly. However, the secret of an effortless, trouble-free click is to pull the elbow back in one smooth, continuous movement, without any stoppage whatsoever, when you know that the sight pin has stopped on the gold. Once started, the elbow should **never stop moving.**

If your form sets the point of the arrow one-eighth inch or more under the clicker, and you pull it out non-stop, the arrow will take less than two seconds to click. And, if you start pulling the instant the sight pin stops on the gold, your form will be as relaxed as it should be; but if you hold for a long period, trying to be too careful, you'll have tensed up in your effort to keep the pin on the gold. That tension will change the direction the arrow will take.

There are other ways to make the clicker work for you, but I have the best luck with this method. It's simple, and it works. If you're having clicker problems you might give it a try.

Thinking is like loving and dying — each of us must do it for ourself.

Relaxed release prevents sore fingers, gives a better release

Several months ago I had a student who was seeking help in his efforts to relieve the pain of a sore third finger. He complained that although he had tried several solutions, nothing seemed to help. His tab covered his fingers completely; his 36-pound bow was not too heavy. He shot with a side-of-the-chin anchor, using a 10-strand Dacron string.

His question to me was, would it help the situation to use a 14- or 16-strand string?

I had to admit that the larger string would help the sore finger to some extent, but I didn't think it was the way to approach the problem. A larger string coming off the fingers would make a larger loop toward the

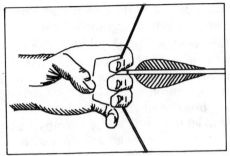

• *Above, a "relaxed" release with the back of the hand properly vertical and hand and forearm in line will prevent sore fingers and give a smoother release. There is little or no string hand torque. Below, a turned hand, away from vertical, creates torque that can result in sore first and/or third fingers.*

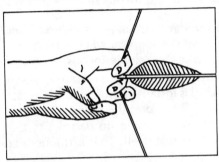

WRONG

shooter's body. This would not help anyone whose string touched the body at full draw. It would also slow the speed of the arrow to some extent.

Although some people are more susceptible to soreness than others, the fact remains that if mistreated, all flesh will respond with blisters, callouses and soreness.

I don't think the smallness of the string is ever the reason for a sore third finger. To help the problem, we must back up farther than that and analyze the shooter's form in that area to find and correct the problem.

Everyone knows that constant, relentless pressure of the string as it leaves the finger tips makes the fingers sore simply because they are not getting out of the way fast enough, and the string scrubs hard as it passes. Since no one can open the fingers faster than the string pressure is pushing, we must find a way to release the fingers from the string in a manner that will minimize the problem.

A great many people will say that to get the arrow on its way, you must turn the string loose. I take exception to that because to turn the string loose you must use and control muscles to open the fingers, and no one can open the fingers, with muscles, fast enough to keep the pressure of the string from scrubbing the tips as it passes. The next step then would be to get fingers open fast enough so that the scrubbing action would be eliminated, to a great extent.

That brings us to the relaxed release.

I teach that the proper and consistent way to send a string on its way is

Best Form

to refuse to hold it. This method has nothing to do with turning the string loose and, in fact, it is the exact opposite of turning it loose.

To refuse to hold, you simply relax the muscles that you are using to hold the string. To understand what I mean, hold a book in your hand between thumb and fingers with the back of your hand up and your arm extended from your body. Do not open the fingers with any muscle whatsoever. The book falls because you relaxed your hand when you refused to hold it. If you use muscle to let the string go, by opening the fingers you can, and sometimes will, open one finger ahead of the other or hold one longer than the others, which are inconsistencies that we cannot see.

These variations show up the most under tournament pressure. After you have mastered the art of the relaxed release, you will not relax one finger ahead of another enough to make the release inconsistent.

There is nothing complicated about it. The reason this release works so well is because the relaxing of the hand is instantaneous, which is as fast or faster than the action of the string. Therefore, the string flips three completely relaxed fingers out of the way causing no damage to the fingers and no inconsistencies in the release itself. That is the perfect release.

I have never been able to teach anyone to relax the fingers that are under the pressure of the bow at full draw. However, I have no trouble getting fingers relaxed by teaching them to relax the **back** of the hand.

The relaxed release is not a cure for all sore finger problems. It may work perfectly, yet the total release effort can be loused up by some other part of the form.

One such third-finger killer that is overlooked by many is the torque of the drawing hand. Everyone torques the drawing hand to some extent at full draw. Some shooters do it excessively, causing severe pressure on the third finger.

Try this. You will see what I mean. Hold the side of your hand at the anchor point on your face with the back of the hand turned up (horizontally). This is the most comfortable position for the hand because it is a natural position. Now, turn your hand down, to make the back of your hand vertical, and you have the position in which you hold the string at full draw. Note that this position feels unnatural and requires concentrated muscle control to hold it there.

And that's where the problem is. The shooter's hand at full draw instinctively wants to twist up into the horizontal position which would feel more natural. This twisting movement, called torque, puts a sideways pressure on the third finger, which can really get scrubbed as it comes off, especially if the fingers at release were not relaxed.

If you have this twisting problem and your finger is not sore, the chances are that your third finger is just resting against the string and is not hooked around it.

Another byproduct of this twisting movement is a sore first finger where it touches the nock. When the twist occurs, the tip of the first finger is pointed down against the nock, which is enough to make it sore. Then it gets another jolt on release as it passes over the nock.

This twisting pressure must be avoided as much as possible. The cure is simple. Just teach yourself that you will keep the back of your hand in the vertical position as you hold the string at full draw, and that you will leave it in that position all the way through the follow-through.

The success or failure of your efforts will hinge on the follow-through.

A good, relaxed release and a minimum of twist (torque) in the string hand will produce no sore fingers.

Is your release the culprit?

If you go up the shooting line and ask everyone what is bothering them the most today, or what's the worst thing about their shooting form, 90 percent of them will tell you their release is the big one.

Why is that? It certainly cannot be true.

I think it's because the release is the only moving part of the explosion of the shot that everyone **sees.** Their attention is thus always called to the release.

Everyone, including people you don't even know and who don't know you, is **conscious** of release. For instance, when someone walks up to you and tells you something about your form when he shouldn't, it's generally or always your release he'll talk about. People won't see or understand the reasons you put other parts of your shot together, but they sure do notice your release.

Concentrated follow through

Follow through is simply keeping concentration until and after the arrow hits. Proper concentration begins with the preparation of the shot and continues unbroken until after the arrow hits.

You can mistakenly believe that the arrow leaves the string so fast that a little break in concentration of 70 milliseconds won't matter — but it will.

When you're on the shooting line, you're concentrating to center the sight in the gold. You have to continue to concentrate as your subconscious gives the command to release, and you must continue concentrating through the explosion and follow through. You can't break the concentration you had when you centered the sight on the target.

But many excellent shooters do, and that's why they don't become champions. There are people on every top line who can outshoot the champion. However, let me reiterate what one champion said to me six or seven years ago: "There are a lot of people on this line who can outshoot me, but they don't know how."

That's what started me thinking more strongly about the "understanding" factor in winning archery. All champions have hangups, but they understand them.

If you are concentrated as you should, someone could hold a gun five feet from you and fire it without your knowing it. You **can** concentrate like that. You do it all the time on plenty of different subjects. It could be deathly quiet on the shooting line, but if someone dropped something with a crash, you might hear it but you wouldn't react until after you've completed the shot. Then you'd simply ask "What was the commotion?" That's all the further it would intrude on you.

Now you can see why there are two kinds of follow through — physical and mental. Most often, shooters see only the physical follow through, to their dismay.

Getting the right rhythm

I'd been worrying and worrying about something, then I finally figured it out. To test it, I started right off with my first student of that particular day, an 11-year-old kid.

"I'll tell you what I want," I said. "I want you to step up to the line but don't shoot until the whistle blows. I'm going to blow the whistle. You're going to shoot three arrows and then step back, because you can shoot only three arrows at a time in the competition we're practicing for.

"So walk up there and straddle the line. Put the arrow in the bow, set the bow on your toe like practically everyone does or lean it on the stabilizer. Then close your eyes and don't open them until the whistle blows. When it does, raise the bow, put your fingers on the string, look up at the target and draw. Prepare the shot, aim, shoot and follow through.

"At the end of the follow through, bring your eyes directly from the target back to your quiver. Pull out the arrow, load the bow with that arrow, raise the bow, draw, aim and shoot. Then do it a third time.

"After that, bring your vision back to the line, step off the line.

"All you will be seeing are the target or the mechanics of loading the bow, preparing the shot and aiming."

The student did that. Then we would talk or joke for a little while, until I'd say, "Ok, it's time to get back up on the line."

I'd blow the whistle again and the student would repeat the procedure three times. I'd be sure to emphasize that he looked **only** at the target or at the mechanics of setting up the shot and then doing it.

"I don't want you to know what color shoes the person next to you on the line is wearing," I'd say, or something like that.

(Later, I didn't insist they close their eyes. They could keep them open, as long as they just looked at the grass at their own feet.)

Remember, they were shooting three arrows with no waiting between each arrow. Absolutely no waiting. Just bing, bing, bing.

I timed all the students without their knowing it. The longest it took any of them to shoot three arrows was 45 seconds. Most of them finished in around 35 seconds.

I had emphasized from the first that I didn't want them to hurry, didn't want them to feel as if they had to hurry. Also, not to put the shot together in a hurry. Be sure the shot is well prepared and feel comfortable with all the elements.

It worked for every one of them. They all got into a smoother rhythm. It also helped their concentration, which in turn helped their shooting.

The next time you get a chance, watch the line. You will see shooters release the arrow, set the bow down and look here or look there or watch the cars going by or an airplane flying overhead or whatever. They're 10,000 miles from archery. And then they'll load another arrow, set up the shot and hold and hold and hold before releasing it, unless the light turns from green to yellow. Then they can get things done fast.

One other aspect ties in with this — when your sight stops the first time in the gold, you shoot. You have your shot prepared so well that you're ready to shoot right now.

Three seconds are all you need, and buddy, that makes smaller groups.

I had a student who said he couldn't shoot the three arrows as I asked.

"Why not?"

"Because I get too tired by the time I get to the third arrow, and I begin to shake."

I said he was blowing smoke, and he said he ought to know about himself pretty well. So I told him to go ahead, but the first time do as I asked and then after that he could do as he preferred.

Without his knowing it, I timed him . . . the time he was using muscles, from the instant he began his draw until the time he released. He is a good one, regarding getting rid of the arrow as soon as the sight stops in the gold.

When he finished I asked, "Are you tired?"

"Boy, I sure am," he said.

"You sure tire easily."

"You would too if you had to shoot that way."

"I wouldn't either."

"Why not."

"Because I'd tell myself I wasn't, for one thing. Now tell me this — how long can you use your muscles without their getting tired," I asked.

He didn't know.

"How long do you think you used your muscles for those three shots?"

He didn't know that either.

"Well," I said, "I timed you with a stopwatch. On the first shot, you took four seconds from the time you began to draw until you released. On the second shot, you took six seconds. On the third shot, you took five seconds. In 15 seconds you're tired?"

He had to laugh. Then he said, "No, I don't think so."

So he thought that over, and he put it to use. Now he doesn't shake any more. He doesn't complain any more.

He's got the rhythm.

Some shooters will say they couldn't speed up, that that wouldn't be their rhythm. I don't buy that. You can learn a rhythm; you learned the one you're using now, didn't you? Maybe the rhythm you now use is good for you, but maybe there's a better rhythm for you. For most everyone, that would be a faster rhythm.

Holding and holding and holding at full draw is either an excuse to delay the inevitable (which means you're not all that confident that your shot is going to hit gold) or that you're trying too hard to put the sight in the gold. Or, rather, **stop** it in the gold. That's what most people reply when I ask about it.

Well, if you're trying to stop it, after you stop it what are you waiting for? The longer you hold, the more strength you use, the more fatigued you become.

When you complain about something, you are taking away some of the sharp edge of your confidence.

Your movies won't lie

Many of you have a movie camera — 8mm or Super 8. Most of you, if you don't have one, can borrow one or rent one from a camera shop.

All of you could help your shooting techniques by watching a few feet of film of yourselves in the act of shooting. They say in newspaper parlance that one picture is worth 10,000 words. I don't think anyone could seriously argue with that, and I know that a motion picture of yourself while shooting will sometimes (most times) show you something you are surprised to find out — something you are so sure you are **not** doing, but there it is. Or something you are so sure that you **are** doing, and there it is **not**.

I have a Bolex camera and projector. Sometimes students will want a picture of themselves in action to keep and review and to pinpoint their progress. They bring a roll of film and we take 50 feet of action. They then have a record they can look at when they want to, and even years later it will be a joy and perhaps a laugh to get out the film just to see how they did it way back when.

Some students are more serious than others. I taught one such person. He wanted a film for several reasons. One, he wanted to see himself as he was then shooting; two, he wanted to study with me all the things we could see happening in his form so he could better understand what he was really supposed to be doing and why.

It was a great idea.

We ran that film forward, backward and in slow motion so many times it should have been worn out. This student shoots much better now because he understands what he is supposed to be doing, what he looks like while doing it, how it feels when he does it. Now in his mind's eye he can see what to do and how to do it.

We took another 50 feet three months after the first and even I was impressed with the progress he had made. Working with a student constantly, you know where the improvements are; but when you compare films taken three months apart, progress stands out.

We studied the second film thoroughly, marked progress and three months later shot film number three. Again we marked progress. To his surprise, he found that a whole new concept of shooting technique was unfolding for him. He was now beginning to see and understand what the coach sees and attempts to pass on to the student. He began to understand the importance of things so small that although the coach had explained them in detail many times, he had never absorbed those small items until he saw himself performing.

Here is another example, involving a woman I had coached for three full years. I had never been able to get her to shoot the kind of smooth release I like my students to have. No amount of work could produce it, although she worked very hard at it. Since she could not make it work, we perfected what she had and got on with it.

Quite by accident, I showed her a film of her shooting. About halfway through, she asked if that was her regular release.

I said yes.

She took her bow, and 12 arrows later, with no help from me, she had a beautiful, relaxed release. She still has it.

What happened?

In this case, one look was worth 10,000 tells. Not until she saw the way she was doing it did she understand how her coach really wanted her to perform it.

It is not out of line here to say that most of you can have 50 feet of film taken of yourself while shooting. In the first place, a camera and projector need not cost all that much, and a friend would probably agree to shoot some footage of you with your film. For the good it will do you, equipment is not too expensive to rent.

Regarding what pictures to take, just remember that you do not need a full-length shot of the subject unless, of course, you want to show an overall view.

Most of the time, you will need only a close-up, depending on which phase of the form you want to study. A study from the waist up, including both the bow and the drawing arm elbow, taken from three angles, makes good study pictures.

Take one study facing the shooter (both of you on the shooting line). Step to the right, take another view standing in front of the bow and two feet from the path of the arrow. Step to the left at about the same angle for the third study.

Of course, there are other angles to shoot, but some are misleading when you view the results. There is a lot of information in the filming angles given here.

Remember, you do not waste film by filming from the start of preparing the shot unless that is not what you want to see. Let's say you want to study release. Start filming just before you think the shooter is going to release and then stop until the next release. You can get a lot of releases on 15 feet of film, and you can bet that inconsistent form will show up.

Use your spotting scope tripod when taking these study pictures. A handheld camera is not very good because you are looking for fine movements in the form; camera movement might say it wrong.

Do not — **do not** — be reluctant to shoot footage. If you are going to study form, footage is the cheapest way to get information. George Helwig, JOAD director and former NAA president, taught me a lesson when he said "Shoot pictures; you pass this way only once."

Now my final bit of advice on making movies.

If you do not intend to take your film and wear it out running it forward, backward, seeing the same thing again and again, analyzing every inch, comparing each shot with the next one, looking for you-know-not-what, then do not waste your money. And remember, this film is no production for you to look pretty in. This film is supposed to be a down-to-earth, working film, showing whatever there is to show **unposed, untouched and honest.**

Profit from it.

If you don't know where you're going, any road will take you there.

Chapter Four: Turning Negatives to Positives

Psyching to win?

I teach my students that if I thought they had to psych out someone to win, then I don't want to coach them. If you have to do that, you haven't won a thing. Instead, the other person simply has lost.

If you want to win, get up there on the line and shoot your best and hope the other archers do, too. If you then have the highest score, you've won something.

Yes, the cheering section is important and beautiful, providing it cheers. It is a form of psyching. I realize a lot of people don't know they're often giving negative things to the shooter when they're trying to be helpful.

I also know that some shooters have to come off the line and complain about how they're shooting. Griping often is nothing more than a shooter's way of looking for support on his problems, real or imagined, so he has a ready excuse when his score doesn't win.

Everyone is different. Everyone handles the positive and negative aspects differently. Some people can talk about anything when they're off the shooting line, then return to 100 percent concentration when they step to the line again. Others cannot do that.

You need to know yourself well enough to know how to handle those situations to your advantage, to relax when you're supposed to relax, to build on positive things, to concentrate when you need to concentrate, to shoot your best.

Use anticipation right

You can anticipate yourself clear out of the ballpark.

You can sit around home and start anticipating and anticipating. The good times roll, victory after victory comes floating in your mental window and into your trophy case. You anticipate a 1,396 FITA.

Then you go to practice, or to the tournament, or anywhere to shoot, and you know, deep down, that you're not even getting close to anything like that score of 1,396. So right away everything falls apart, and then feeling sorry for yourself becomes the greatest sport in the world.

It's easy to feel sorry for yourself then.

What was practiced? Mistakes were practiced, that's what, and then you went home and said "I've been out practicing."

Anticipation can be **good** for you, though. If you don't anticipate, you're going to the shooting line like a piece of stone. You've got to see yourself on the first target. You've also got to be rational enough to know that you're **building up to it,** and today might be the day! I don't believe you can get to the line and say "Today is the day." Maybe a few of the very top shooters can, but they've worked for it and experienced success. They know the odds are probably more in their favor than in most other shooters' favor.

You have to think success. It all has to be kept in perspective; you can't lie about it to yourself or to anyone. You can't expect more than you're capable of, but you always have to think you're more capable than you are.

Priority action must reflect priority thoughts

I believe most archers have **not** thought about their general archery priorities enough to have them spelled out and in order. Actually, you may not know whether you have priorities or whether you don't. And that tends to muddy the water.

For instance, the yellow light can change your priorities in a hurry. It does just that for plenty of shooters. This is mentioned elsewhere in the book, but I state it again here because it is important.

You shoot the first arrow, but then further shooting seems to be placed on hold. You draw and let down, draw and let down, draw and let down until that yellow light comes on. Then you can make two shots in 20 seconds just as slick as can be, and they will be good shots.

Your priorities changed, probably from trying to pull the arrow through the clicker to beating the yellow light. It suddenly is no problem to pull through the clicker.

You also miss priorities when you start worrying about your tackle. You ought to know that it is right and put your priority on placing your shots where you know and believe they should be.

I have to ask students every once in a while "What do you want to do?" A lot of times I'll be a bit exasperated with the student because they'll seem to be practicing without a purpose.

"What are you trying to do?"

"I'm trying to shoot better," they reply.

"Well, then, why don't you listen to what I'm telling you? Try some of these items," I say.

All this shows is that they had their priorities wrong, weren't concentrating on the right things and didn't actually hear what I had said. They may have **thought** they heard what I said, and they may have **thought** they understood what I said, but I can see they did not simply because they haven't put to use anything I suggested.

The reason a coach often needs to chide, insult, brow beat or coax a student in this area is because he **doesn't realize** he has his priorities out of whack. He thinks they're organized, but his thoughts are misleading him.

What does he think? He thinks "I want to shoot. I'm in a tournament, and I want to win it."

Then when he or she **does** get up to the line, his thoughts are not in the right order because his priorities are out of line. He's seeing that glorious finish without paying proper attention to the work it takes to get there. He's blinded by his own thoughts of glory.

As a result, he's not fulfilling his responsibilities to himself. His responsibility is to determine and set priorities, to set an attainable goal, then understand what he has to do to reach that goal. So many shooters don't understand what they're supposed to do, never come to grips with the work it takes to become a champion.

There are no easy answers, just one heck of a lot of hard work.

Accept responsibility, don't pass the buck

When I get a chance to talk about that great human game called "passing the buck," I get right up on a soapbox and cut loose.

Passing the buck — refusing to accept blame or responsibility — is the biggest doggone cop-out there ever was.

If you, as a shooter or as a person, can't stand up and take your licks, you aren't going to be the champion you want to be. You don't have the necessary confidence in yourself. Nor have you developed the intestinal fortitude, otherwise known as guts.

I'd rather a person be confused. But one who deliberately passes the buck all the time, as far as I'm concerned, he or she isn't going to get anywhere. In fact, I **know** that person won't rise above mediocrity or just slightly above average at best.

How and where do archers pass the buck?

In everything. Excuses here . . . pass it on there to something or to someone. It's not their fault. Nothing is ever their fault. They can shoot three tens and shoot one in the seven, and it isn't their fault. Their arm did it, not them. If they know they flinched, for instance, there'll be a reason. Meaning, of course, they will explain it and it won't even be close to a reason — but it will be an explanation.

It's a refusal to be honest with yourself, a refusal to accept the fact that you're going to make mistakes, and then to accept those mistakes. The only difference is that the pass-the-buck artist never makes mistakes. If you don't believe him, ask him.

The wall of rationalization

I sometimes feel like giving awards to the experts at rationalization. Such a shooter always has an answer, a reason, for everything you ask him or her. I don't know how to talk with or help someone who is a past master at that because there's an impenetrable wall between us and between that shooter and the truth. That shooter may never have thought of a reason something didn't work, until you asked about it; but you can be guaranteed that the shooter will have an answer and will be emphatic and positive in his or her statement of that reason. He or she is conning himself or herself worse than anyone else is being conned.

Being rational and thinking irrational are about as far apart as New York and San Francisco. You might think you're cute as the devil when you're shooting, and you've got everything figured out. You know exactly why this works or that doesn't work. And you keep fooling yourself with it all. I believe that deep down you know or suspect that certain things aren't good, but you rationalize it somehow.

Because you are **not honest** with yourself.

People often perform in a certain manner because they've never learned how **not** to perform that way. For instance, a shooter does a certain thing **only** during a tournament. Only the conditions of the real thing cause the problem.

That can be solved. I believe shooters should try to practice getting into the mood of a tournament. This is truly psyching yourself into something, and in so doing you will find the solution.

I asked a girl one time to try that, because in the previous tournament she had become emotionally upset over an outside influence and her shooting deteriorated. She really lost it.

During a practice session, I asked "Do you remember how you felt the other day at that tournament when you were so emotional?"

"Do I ever!," she said.

"Can you get that emotional again? Right now? Right here?"

"I don't know . . ."

"Put yourself in that tournament again. See if you can become an actress. See if you can get yourself so worked up you start to fall apart like you did in the tournament," I suggested. Let me tell you, this was breaking new ground.

It worked. So help me. She cried. She more than cried, she bawled.

Right there in front of me. It was tremendous, and I was so proud of her.

"What are you going to do to get rid of that? Are you going to relax and have faith?" I asked.

She smiled and said, "Yes, I am."

She did, too. She cleared her emotions, dried her tears and started shooting beautifully. She never had that trouble again because she knew what caused it, that she could handle it — by not allowing it to happen again, and that there was no problem simply because she had maintained control in putting herself through that situation again and coming out of it. She saw the light at the end of the tunnel and came out into that light.

She came to grips with the problem and looked at it, felt it. She discovered all the triggers, the one to become emotional and the one to become unemotional. She knew then that if the problem ever began to arise again in a tournament, she'd be able to say to herself, "I know how to handle that." It wasn't new territory any more.

It is difficult to get people to understand that you have to work at what's wrong **while** it is wrong.

Once again, the whole thing is mental. You have to **understand** the problem to solve it.

Mission Possible: In 10 seconds this shooter will NOT self destruct!

Shooters self destruct. Often enough that it is a problem.

This happens because you, as a shooter, have your priorities out of order and/or don't practice hard enough. You often don't attempt to psych yourself into a better mood. When you get in a down mood, you like to remain there.

You want all the advice everyone can give you, and you think that that's what is needed, but you take none of it. You use every excuse that ever was invented, some of which are so flimsy you embarrass even yourself.

Name anything in the world and you do it.

And the crazy thing is, **you can be innocent of all these things and still do them.** If your psyche says "mold me," and you blindly follow what is given to you, instead of developing the positive control you should have, then you've not been responsible to yourself. You were not anything, just a malleable lump, turning with the direction the wind blew. That certainly isn't good.

So you must avoid self destruction by psyching yourself into shooting better. You are honest with yourself and ask yourself what you are so worked up about. Ask what specifically is keeping you from attaining your goals. Consciously tell yourself you're going to relax, then let your subconscious and conscious do it. If someone said something which upset you, ask yourself why that person and that statement upset you. Ask yourself why you listen to things like that, why you don't concentrate more, etc.

Being honest with yourself is a good way of saying every bit of it. To go with that, you must accept the mistakes you make. If you do those two things, you're well on the way to licking every problem.

Anxiety is solved by honesty

Anxiety bothers many people. Usually they're worried about their tackle. They think something on it needs adjusting or fixing. They spend practically all their **un**conscious time on the question: Is my tackle correct? Others can't ever get comfortable with themselves and their tackle because they worry about their release.

Anxiety will kill you, competitively. It also will kill your enjoyment of archery.

The only way to combat it is to be honest and direct with yourself — "What am I anxious about? Why am I so uptight? I'm hurting myself being this way. Don't I have confidence?"

It's simply a lack of confidence from the beginning, or their confidence has been shaken a bit by something. There's often the feeling that the shooter hasn't brought it with him, that he hasn't yet put it all together or that he left his shot back on the practice butts.

Maybe it is nothing more than a mental distraction, where you would feel anxiety over the solution of another problem unrelated to archery, but which keeps you from concentrating solely on your shooting. You could have had a fight with your spouse last night, or with your parents. Maybe you received a speeding ticket and that's bothering you.

The solution again is simply to be honest with yourself. Are you going to be in control of yourself and do the best you can, or are you not? Be positive, not negative. Concentrate on the strengths in your shooting form and they'll help smooth over the weaknesses. If you do the best you can with the skills you bring to the tournament, there's no reason to feel anxiety. False expectation — thinking you should win when your skill level is not up to it — can create an anxiety that has the weakest reason for existing. The solution is to set and strive for attainable goals, within a time frame that challenges you but does not defeat you. Then you will relax and do your best, which will begin moving you up the ladder of success.

The only walls which are impenetrable are those which you build around yourself.

Control your aggression

Aggression can work both ways — you can be too aggressive, and you can be not aggressive enough.

If you're not aggressive enough, you don't address the problem. That's another way of not being honest with yourself. Outside influences may buffet you. You may seek solutions everywhere but from within yourself. You will have difficulty selecting goals, and if you have no goals, or poorly defined goals, you cannot expect to get anywhere.

If you're too aggressive, you're often too mechanical in much of your problem solving and often impatient. You often want to win without taking all the necessary steps, ie, work, to get you there. You have to take the time to do all the little things which must be done to put your shot together and keep your head screwed on straight. There are no short-cuts, but if you're too aggressive — or impatient — you look for them and end up hurting yourself. You surely won't hurt anyone else.

Shooters have a tendency to over-react to a poor shot. That's like equating a fingernail trimmed too short with cutting off your finger.

I see this a lot in coaching:

"What do you mean, you shot a bad shot?", I ask.

"It just wasn't . . ."

"How bad was it?"

"Well, I just can't say. But it was bad!"

I know darn well the shooter is reacting as if he'd suddenly discovered he'd cut several fingers off his hand, when all he should be reacting to is the fact that he trimmed a fingernail too short. You don't want to trim your fingernail too short because the finger then becomes tender — but if you're reading a book you still can turn the pages with that finger. You certainly did not cut off several fingers.

So it is more an undesirable shot than a bad shot. You have made it, so you accept it. When you have your act together, your aggression will be controlled and positive. You won't have wild swings of emotion or reaction to shots that are less than desired.

Put a face on those fears

The only thing I've told anyone about fear is that you must ask yourself: What am I afraid of?

You can't simply repeat it to yourself. You have to want to know, and so if you will just stand there, or sit there, or whatever, and say to yourself, "I'm scared to death . . ."

I've mentioned this countless times going into a tournament, to my girl students especially. I don't know why them more, but maybe they've been less accustomed to the tension just prior to athletic competitions because there have been fewer situations for them, fewer opportunities for them to become acclimated.

So we just talk it through.

"Okay, let's sit down a minute. What are you scared of?"

"I don't know. I'm just scared."

"Do you know what scared is? You know there has to be a reason. What are you afraid of? What's scaring you?"

Some can tell me, some can't. There often is just a general fear, not accompanied with proper thought to put some shape to it and begin to overcome it. They're scared because they're going into a tournament, but that's not what I'm trying to make them realize. I don't expect them actually to be able to tell me what they're scared of, and that's perfectly normal. We all have nameless, shapeless fears that make us uneasy.

Now, since I don't like to use the word "scared" I just tell them "I don't think you're scared. Do you think you're going to get hurt?" (No.) "What does 'scare' mean to you? Are you sure you're scared or **just concerned**?"

Then they begin to see a way out of the forest.

"Well, I guess maybe concerned would be closer to it."

"I'm **glad** you're concerned. That shows you care, you have desire to do well. I **hope** you're concerned when you go into a tournament. I'm concerned, too, but I'm not going to get uptight over the tournament. I'll take whatever comes; I will accept it. I am concerned that everything will go right, that you and I are trying to do our best, that you will stay cool and calm."

Those are my general comments to a shooter. They will vary from shooter to shooter, of course, depending upon the direction and shape our conversation takes.

All I'm doing is focusing on the subject and being honest with the shooter about it. The shooter gives substance to the nameless dread, and then he or she can deal with it. And in so doing, we turn a negative into a positive, because this becomes one more thing the shooter and I have triumphed over. We have been totally honest with each other and with the fear. "Concern" is a positive word; "fear" is a negative word. There's a world of difference.

Are you organized?

There's organization, and then there's too much organization. I remember a shooter who was so organized that, my word, everything had to be **exactly** this or that, and every little thing had to click. He thought of everything. It took him 10 minutes to shoot an arrow . . . or that's what it seemed like . . . and he never could get very far up the target line.

He lost sight of the objective, and he worried everything to death. He was trying to be perfect, but you can't be perfect.

Obsessive compulsion and parents

Obsessive compulsion is more of a problem with parents than with shooters. Parents can become possessed with their childrens' winning something, to the point that they actually obstruct that child's or those childrens' progress and success.

They push, shove, drive and smother the child. Sure, this can move the child along, but at what cost to the child, at what cost to the parent, at what cost to a good parent-child relationship?

What should a good parent do?

If he or she or they are going to pay for a coach, work with the coach. If the coach says not to push the child, don't push. If the coach says not to nag, don't nag. If the coach advises saying nothing to the child about his or her shooting, say nothing. This may be frustrating to some parents, but they must remember that they and the coach have the child's best interests in mind.

If the coach believes the child needs encouragement, do so actively. Brag about him to himself, to his friends and to your friends. But do it right, don't be false. Falseness may fool someone for a short time, but it won't work for long.

If the child wants to feel sorry for himself, ignore it. However, if he or she is mentally down, and legitimately so, then sympathize and be the understanding parent. But don't overdo it. Don't make a heart transplant out of a sore finger.

The key simply is to communicate with the coach and child and work together.

The coach, of course, has to have the sense to approach each situation correctly. You can't just walk up to parents and say "This is the way I want you to treat your kid."

If coach and parents are really interested in the kid's best interests, they will work together. It's kind of odd to hire a coach and then not work with him or her, but it happens.

Self analysis — how much, how little?

How much self analysis should a shooter do? How good can a shooter be at it? Does self analysis enter into it at all? How much of it is good, how much is bad?

To a great degree, everything we're talking about in understanding winning archery is self analysis. It varies with individuals, in amount and in style. It can be underdone, as we have noted, or it can be overdone.

In accepting mistakes, you accept them as history and go on from there. But you also can be retrospective. You can look back at such an error and learn from it, gain from it. Don't worry about it, just take from it anything which will benefit you in the future.

For instance, when a session is completed and you're back home, look back and assess the day.

All you should do is tell yourself, as an example, "Let's see, I was a little rusty. My release wasn't good today, and I know it wasn't. So I'll improve it."

That's about it. It is positive and constructive.

You're **not** going to say, "What the heck was wrong with me today?"

When you understand the situation and understand yourself, you're on the way to understanding winning archery.

Chapter Five: Equipment, Form and Your Mind

Coach, bow tuner, you — three is *not* a crowd

A man approached me the other day in Encanto Park and said, "I wonder if you would help me with a problem I have developed and can't seem to correct? My arrows sorta wobble in flight, and we can't seem to straighten them out."

I am careful about stating judgmental opinions to someone else's student, so I asked this man who he meant when he said "we."

He told me that Mr. Smith was coaching him but Mr. Jones was tuning his equipment; that Mr. Jones said he should change his hand position on the bow handle so he would get a little more torque which would probably straighten the arrow out.

I asked what Mr. Smith thought about that.

He answered, "Oh, those two guys don't get along too well. Coach says my hand is okay, and I do like it there. My groups are great."

I said, "In that case, why are you worrying over a slight arrow wobble?"

"Well, that's just it," he told me. "Mr. Jones says I had better police up my form if I want good arrow flight, and my coach says that my form is consistent and not causing the arrow to wobble. Both of these men are experts, as you well know, but I am a bit confused, and that's why I'm asking your advice."

I knew what he was talking about. Some people will have anyone change anything at any time to **fix** a wobbly arrow. This they do without consulting anyone as to what might be the reason that individual is shooting that particular form, or what it might do to his groups. It's a mystery to me why some equipment tuners and coaches are reluctant to work together. Each one seems to think what he does is more important than the other, and they sometimes publicly criticize each other's efforts.

Criticism may not be agreeable, but it is necessary. It fulfills the same function as pain in the human body: It calls attention to an unhealthy state of things.
Winston Churchill

They are not thinking. Both are important, and they are important to each other.

Neither one has any control over who the student hires as coach or as equipment tuner, so why can't they act professionally and as a team help produce a winner? If you were a race horse, how much chance would you have to win, place or show if your trainer and your jockey would not cooperate with each other?

The key is to produce for the shooter.

A few of the serious archers, depending upon their motivation, their inherent skill and aptitudes, and their training in other areas of their life, learn to tune their own equipment.

Those shooters who must rely on someone else to tune their equipment should seek out the best, one who can analyze each individual and know what to do. Everything being equal, their bow tuner and their coach, working together, should produce a winner.

In archery, everyone wants his arrows to fly perfectly. And yet, sometimes, circumstances dictate that acceptance of an imperfectly flying arrow is the wise choice. No one should spend days or hours striving desperately to perfect arrow flight, while disregarding everything else.

I saw this happen to a shooter who was shooting better scores than he ever had before, with the same equipment used when he won the world championship. One day his equipment tuner noticed a slight wobble in his arrow flight, caused (in my opinion) by the stiffening of the shooter's release fingers. He immediately (with file and wrench) started changing to take out the wobble. That was the end of that shooter's comeback.

If I were in competition and shooting **good groups** at all distances and someone told me my arrows were wobbling slightly, it wouldn't bother me a bit, especially if the arrows had all been flying straight just a few days before. I hope that I would have the presence of mind to figure out that since I had the same equipment setup, I should relax and put my shot together better. Even if this wouldn't take all the wobble out, I would still be doing what I stepped up to the line to do — grouping my arrows in the place I want them to group.

Gentleman Jim Pickering, my good friend from Utah, told me that he did not care if his arrows turned over and went in the target fletching first, just so they were all touching one another in the target. Jim does not lose tournaments if his arrows happen to wobble **slightly.** He just puts them in the target touching each other and worries later.

I am not advocating the disregarding of bad arrow flight. That would be ridiculous. I do advocate that you use your head and not get carried away, if your arrows are grouping, even though they might wobble **slightly.**

The object of tuning equipment is to make the arrows fly to the target consistently **in a group.** If they do that, a **slight** wobble is **sometimes** of no consequence.

It is a great source of confidence to the shooter when he knows his equipment is well tuned, and his coach and equipment tuner are working together as a team for his benefit. It is a great source of satisfaction to those people when their joint effort produces a winner. Cooperation between all parties will enhance the whole sport of archery.

You don't have to lie awake nights to succeed; just stay awake days.

Turning the clicker key

Should I use a clicker? Should I use it only for a draw check? Will it cause me some kind of trouble later on? Is it hard to learn to use? Will it improve my score?

I think the clicker is a great invention. It is no secret that it has elevated scores a great deal. I most emphatically think it is an aid, beneficial to everyone who understands it enough to use it properly.

I **do** believe that 75 percent of the people shooting with a clicker do not understand much about how it works as an aid.

What can the clicker do for you?

First, it **can** make you shoot better, score better. It **can** make your form better. In fact, if you understand how to really use it, every part of your form will be better.

Great care must be used in setting the clicker in the proper place. I will not allow a student to use one until I am sure that we have his form consistent enough to make it work properly. This is most important if you want to use the clicker as it should be used.

If, and I repeat, **if** your form is good and consistent, set the clicker to that form only. Whatever you do, don't set it any old place and try to pull to it, or set it at a special place just because it looks good. Set it to your form as you always prepare that form for the shot.

You put the shot form together; let someone else mark the end of your arrow and place your clicker there. Now **leave it alone.**

What could possibly be the reason the clicker becomes hard to pull through? You have had your clicker for a couple of weeks and are doing better, but now it is becoming harder to make it click. So you move it out a little. That move outward is the signal for what is coming next — loss of confidence, frustration, lower scores and perhaps a divorce.

Common sense should tell you that if the clicker has not been moved and if you are shooting the same length arrows, then the only thing that has changed is your form. Correct **that;** don't move the clicker.

The same thing happens in reverse. You pull out of the clicker too soon. Perhaps it clicks before you get anchored. Common sense again, whether you like it or not, says the problem is a breakdown in your form. **Leave the clicker alone.**

Let's say that everything stays as it is and you are doing fine, but it slowly becomes harder and harder to pull through the clicker. In fact, it becomes so bad you let down two, three, four times before you get a shot off. When you apply common sense to that one, remember that when the yellow flag comes up and time is running out, you are always able to make it click before the red flag appears.

That, my friend, is also your form (between your ears) that is fouling up the execution of the shot. It is an indicator that is telling you to police **all** your form. It is not necessarily just one thing that is causing 100 percent of the problem.

Let me tell you how I teach the use of a clicker, and why.

First, the clicker is a shooting aid. You don't have to have it to shoot well. I get very upset when it becomes something you think you just have to use or you cannot shoot.

I want you to learn, believe and understand that you are not trying to pull an arrow out from behind something. You are trying to **hear** a clicker click, so you can get on with the explosion part of the shot.

To do this you simply move the elbow of the pulling arm backward.

That's all you think about and that's all there is to it. You learn one little habit that produces the click you want to hear.

To some of you, that is so simple you won't believe it or even try it. You will insist on pulling an arrow out from behind a piece of metal that is attached to the sight window of your bow. Whether you know it or not, you will be waiting and wondering where the point of the arrow is? How much farther must you pull? Why doesn't the damned thing click? So you panic and can't think how to get it done.

I say that you are working on the problem from the wrong end. All you want or need is to hear a click. Forget about the mechanics of what is going to cause it to click. That should be a simple habit to learn.

This is not the only way to make a clicker click. You can push your bow arm toward the target and make it work.

In my opinion, this is not so good since I believe the bow arm unit is the most important part of the shooting form and is susceptible to many minute variations that can throw the arrow off. I do not want the bow arm tampered with in any manner, including pushing.

You can also make the clicker click by tightening the string fingers slightly. This, in my opinion, takes away from my idea of a good setup for a smooth, relaxed release and is hard to execute consistently. Another drawback in this method is that it is in reality a triggered release which you make happen when you want to.

The whole idea of using a clicker properly is that the clicker should never be anticipated. **If it is perfectly executed the click will be a surprise,**

a complete surprise. The shot will explode in perfect harmony of motion because without any anticipation you have not tensed up anywhere in your form.

It is so simple and easy to use a clicker. If it is so easy, why is it so hard for me to make it work? you ask.

As I have said before, I think we work on the wrong end or part of the setup.

Most clicker shooters keep worrying (knowingly or unknowingly) about the mechanics of what makes the clicker work. Is every mechanical part of this thing going to perform when and how it should?

You don't worry about what the mechanics are or do when you start your car. You turn the key which makes electricity flow to the starter which turns the shaft that pushes the gear to engage the flywheel that turns the engine so the sparkplug can spark which causes the explosion that starts your car. All you do is turn the key. You don't worry about the mechanics.

Forget about the clicker mechanics. Concentrate on turning the **clicker key,** which is a slight backward movement of the elbow.

Give it a chance

When a shooter is looking for an excuse, you'll often hear him or her say, "My bow hand doesn't feel right," or "My release isn't smooth enough," or any of a hundred different things of equipment or form.

Maybe they are having a bit of a problem, and maybe they do have a good idea what the reason for the problem may be . . . but, also, one of the biggest reasons they may be having a problem is that they don't leave the questioned item in their form alone long enough for it to become a habit. They don't give it a chance either to prove or disprove itself. They don't give their subconscious and muscle memory a chance to develop a habit by feel.

Advantages of a bow sling

A spectator walked up to me at a tournament and asked if all those gadgets the shooters were using on their equipment were really necessary? I thought the question was a good one, and I told him so.

This gentleman had asked specifically about the bow sling. He had observed that there were three distinct types in use at this tournament and he wanted to know the differences or if there were reasons for the differences.

I explained that there were two distinct reasons for the sling, the obvious being to keep the bow from falling to the ground if the shooter's hand was relaxed enough through the shot to let it go. His remark was that it seemed silly to him. If you had the bow in your hand, why couldn't you grab it and hold on to keep it from falling?

Well, he has a point there, so I asked him to step over in the shade, and I tried to enlighten him on the fact that archery has come of age and is no longer the step-child of sports.

I was proud to point out that archery as a competitive sport was included for the first time in the 1972 Olympics in Munich, Germany, and that the United States took the men's and women's gold medals. This feat was repeated at the 1976 Games in Montreal, Canada.

I also pointed out that the improvement of the sport and the steady advance of the scores was a direct result of trial and error experimentation by the shooters, and the so-called gadgets he was asking about were three different ideas on how to keep you from grabbing the bow on the shot and prevent possible harm to the bow if it fell to the ground.

His statement that you could grab it and hold on without a gadget prompted me to explain in detail the **other** reason for the sling's use and my opinion of which sling was the most advantageous to the shooter and why.

Bow sling number one attaches to the bow below the handle. A leather strap goes up over the wrist and can be adjusted for length. **Bow sling number two** is a braided rope type with a loop around the wrist and the loose end going around the bow between the first and second finger with a hook on the end of it that hooks into the loop around the wrist. **Bow sling number three** is called a finger sling. It can be of leather, rope or cord. It has two loops. One fits around the first finger, the other around the thumb. This sling loops around the front of the bow.

In my opinion, **number two is the best all-around sling** and advantageous to the most archers. All three will keep the bow from falling to the ground; however, there are some side effects that need to be considered.

Number 1 and Number 3 make you mentally prepare to grab the bow before the arrow has left the string. When your brain gives the command for the fingers to let the string go, your bow hand also knows the shock is coming. At that precise moment — before your string fingers even leave your anchor — your bow hand and bow hand fingers start to react, which is too soon.

If you're confident the bow won't do anything wrong (such as jump from your hand), your bow hand won't react when you give the release command to your string fingers. It's a defensive technique, and that's why I talk about it. In this instance, I coach defensive technique for positive results. It's what the sling makes you do or allows you not to do that is important.

As we know, the bow jumps forward toward the target when the string is released. In my opinion, that forward movement must not be impaired in any manner until the arrow has cleared the string. I must assume that the shooter's bow hand will be so relaxed that it will follow that forward movement, allowing the sling to stop that movement after the arrow has cleared the string.

If sling number one is a bit too tight, the forward motion of the bow will be impaired when the bow hits the sling which is attached to the bow below the handle. If the bow hand is as completely relaxed as it should be, the bow will end up hanging halfway to the ground, which is not good for anyone's composure.

Bow sling number two can be minutely adjusted to fit any individual need. Since the sling goes around the bow high up on the handle between the first and second finger of the hand, the forward movement of the bow disturbing the arrow if the sling was too short would be all but eliminated. The drop of the bow toward the ground because of a completely relaxed hand would also be taken care of because the sling contacts high on the handle, not below it. It is a good one.

Sling number three is the most perfect one as far as slings go, but for some shooters it can, and too often does, have a side effect that is hard to find and cope with. It has no adjustment other than tying a knot in it, which generally makes it much too short.

If you use this type, select or make one that is just the right length for stopping the forward bow movement after the arrow has cleared the string, but not so loose that the bow will drop through the hand. Your hand can catch on the sight, which is painful. This sling contacts the bow high up on the handle in the center of the bow. This takes away the chance of tilting the bow with a tight sling.

Although I like this sling, I seldom recommend it because it is so easy for a shooter to develop trouble with grouping and never be able to put the blame where it belongs. In fact many shooters hardly believe that it is important enough to cause trouble, but I can assure you it is.

When the shock of the bow is felt going forward against this piece of material fastened to our thumb and first finger, the natural thing to do is to raise the thumb and finger to keep it from pulling off, even though we know it is tightly attached and will not come off on impact. Since the thumb and finger always know when the mind triggers the release of the string, they anticipate the impact and start their movement too soon, which also moves the hand. This anticipation and movement of thumb and finger before the arrow has left the string can be, and many times is, the direct cause of groups opening up for no apparent reason. Most

---

Take a good look at yourself. You're someone's impression of archery.

---

finger sling shooters don't think they have this problem. I hope they don't.

The spectator called the sling a gadget. To some it may be. To me it is one of the many things which have helped the shooter perfect his shooting skills and raise his scores.

Fixing the trouble

If you don't know what the trouble is, how can you fix it?

You can't. So forget about it and trust the skills which got you there.

One time years ago I was field captain at a national tournament. George Clauss was fighting for the lead but suddenly went five points down. I had to go to a supply trailer to get something, and I passed George. He was standing in the shade, relaxing and having a soda.

"How you doing, George," I asked, mostly to be sociable.

"Ahh, I've lost it," he said, meaning that he had trouble with something in his shooting form.

"What's the matter?" I asked.

"I don't know. But it'll straighten out," he said.

Later, on the line, I walked past him and asked how things were.

He smiled and said, "I got it back."

He did, but not soon enough to regain the lost points. But I think that's tremendous. He didn't know what to fix, but he didn't worry about it. He believed in himself and his skills.

Now I have a trick question I ask when I'm asking a lot of questions. I'll say, "You've practiced up to the state championship, and you're still hot. You were ahead of everyone, but about halfway through the tournament suddenly your arrows begin to scatter. You don't know why. You'd get some high lefts now and then. Now . . . my question is . . . what would you do? What part of your form would you correct to eliminate that?"

Only twice have I been answered correctly. The answer, of course, is: "If I don't know what's wrong, I can't fix it."

A sobering thought

When a shooter begins to worry about his or her tackle, I always stress one thing —

Any matched bow and arrow tackle setup is capable of shooting far better than you are capable of making it shoot.

Chapter Six: Blazing a Tournament Trail

Steps on your tournament preparation ladder

I think that preparation is the key to success in all things. Small details can, and do, make or break any endeavor, and archery competition is no exception to that rule.

How do you prepare yourself for the grind of archery competition? Have you all the information you need?

Where, exactly, will the tournament be held? How will you get there? What round will be shot, what time does it start and when will it be over? Have you made the necessary arrangements for feeding the dog or cat while are gone, receiving your mail and watering the lawn? Do you have arrangements for a babysitter at the tournament or will you take the girl next door along to do the job?

Do you need to clear this trip and the time you'll be gone with your employer so there will be no problems when you return? Is your car in good shape and has it been completely serviced and ready to go?

Is your tackle really tuned as it should be so you are satisfied with the setup? Do you have extra bowstrings that have been tested and shot in so they will shoot like the old one. Are your arrows in good shape, and do you have enough ready to take with you to last through any accident? Is your tab ok, and do you have a spare one all trimmed and broken in so you know it shoots ok, just in case you need it? Have you inspected your armguard lately to see if it has a good, hard, smooth surface, should the string (accidentally) hit it?

Are you disgusted because you don't feel that you are in good shape for this competition, or did you practice enough so you think you are in good shape for it? Does your coach think you are ready?

Have your current "pressing problems" been resolved to the point where you are at peace with yourself in regard to them? Do you think this tournament will be a good one? Do you think it is worth the trip? If not, why are you going?

Do you have emergency cash on hand and are your credit cards all in order and paid up?

Did you pre-register and send in your money far enough ahead of time to assure you of a spot on the line when you get there?

Are you mentally prepared to shoot confidently in **any kind of weather?** If there is a possibility of rain, wind or cold weather, have you actually practiced shooting a round in the rain with a wet tab? Have you made a point of shooting a practice round when the wind is really blowing, to develop your own way to cope? Do you know whether you can shoot with a heavy coat on? Have you tried it and found out what adjustments, if any, you will have to make?

What about people, personalities, character quirks and maddening habits? Is there any one person that you hope will not show up at the shoot? Will it bother you very much if he or she does? If this person was assigned to your target, would you ask to be moved to another target? What if someone on your target has a bothersome habit, like cracking his knuckles every time before he nocks an arrow, or slapping his leg with the arrow every time he takes one from the quiver? Would **you** do something about it? Does it bother you if your wife or husband or anyone else stands and watches you shoot? Does it bother you if that person is shooting higher scores than you do?

This question barrage could go on and on without covering all the small details that are so important to the success of a competitive shooter. My reason for listing so many of these things was to start you thinking about your own personal list of details. Many of the items are so commonplace we often tend to pass over them lightly without making definite decisions or disposing of specific matters long before leaving home for the tournament site.

If you plan to shoot in a tournament and expect to do well, there will be a list of things that need attention and **must** be taken care of **before** competition begins. You must be at peace with yourself and the world!

After you are conscious of this inner relaxation, **then** you can go on and psych yourself up for the shoot in whatever is the right way for you. I think all good shooters in some way and to some degree do this. I can't give you here a bonafide, no-fail formula for doing this, but I can mention a thing or two which may be all the help you need to see more clearly the path you should follow to put yourself in the winner's circle. **You,** of course, are the only one who can do that.

If you want to be a winner in the next tournament you attend, first sit down in a quiet place and have a talk, a very serious talk, with yourself about what your actual, basic problems are, and **then** come to grips with what seems to cause these problems.

Too many wishful winners stop at the point where they recognize their problems. It is good to know your problems, but if you are going to be true winner material, you will not stop the thought process until you have determined the probable **cause** of said problem or problems so it or they can then be eliminated.

It is at this point of training that many a potential champion is lost. Too many of us today are too soft in the self-discipline department. It is a rough hurdle and, in my opinion, causes more trouble than anything else. It is the failure of an individual to face facts as they are, to point the finger of blame at himself or herself, if that is where the fault lies.

Any archer training to become a winner will have to accept the truth of this statement and then act accordingly, **every time** he or she is shooting in competition! Any contestant's score is not determined so much by circumstances and the actions of others as it is by **his own reactions** to those actions and circumstances!

Pearl Bailey told Johnny Carson one night, in answering a question, that other singers did not bother her at all, **because she did not allow them** to bother her! That was a championship answer!

At a recent tournament, a man was complaining about another man standing right behind him when the first man was shooting on the line.

He said, "It just bugs me when he stands there like that."

"Why does it bug you?"

"I don't know, but it **does.**"

If he had faced up to the whole truth he would have seen that he was **allowing** it to bug him. He was reacting poorly to another's actions. With practice, and in time, that same man could train himself to completely block out that episode.

Follow-through is as important in mental preparation for competition as it is in the literal shooting of an arrow. You must practice your decisions on the shooting line, without exception. Don't expect perfection from yourself, however, when you are first starting on a program like this. This is a cultivated frame of mind that pays high dividends.

I really believe you should do a lot of **thinking things over** every time before you go to a shoot. What kind of things? All kinds of things involving preparation. Material, mechanical and mental preparation! Think through a schedule of all things both great and small that you will need to take care of **before** the opening of the tournament, putting each one in its proper spot. Make any decisions that must be made and then follow through on them **now** instead of leaving them until the last minute. Eliminate, as far as possible, anything and everything that could cloud your mind or even give it a controversial thought on the day of competition.

On the night before the shoot, and just before you go to bed, take a few minutes to recall the burning desire you had to shoot in this tournament, and now here you are! Relish for a minute the joy of anticipation. **You** are ready for competition! You will go out in the morning and shoot your very best just for the sheer pleasure of shooting a higher score than someone else because you **know** you can.

If you **always** shoot your **best** you have no way to go but up, so you will send each and every arrow on its way with the skill, grace and precision that a beautifully straight, perfectly matched arrow deserves. The time you spent on preparation is beginning to pay off. You feel so good! No doubt about it, you **can** and **will** be among **the winners!**

> **As you strive to improve yourself, remember that even if you are on the right track you will be run over if you just sit there.**

Increase practice before a tournament?

Suppose a shooter knows his or her muscle tone is good enough to carry through a tournament without fatigue. Is there any need for him or her to increase practice time as the tournament draws near?

I don't believe so. You can only build a good thing so far.

In fact, I don't like to see a shooter shooting anything right before a tournament. If I had six people and complete control over them, I wouldn't let them shoot an arrow for two days before the tournament.

For three reasons:

1) Their muscles already would be toned;

2) They would be so eager to get at it that they would approach the line with joy;

3) They're not mentally fatigued, but refreshed. Their mental state is honed to a fine edge and they're ready to go.

But I confine myself, with my students, to telling them I don't want them shooting the day before the tournament. If I get an argument, my answer is this: "If you're not ready one day before a tournament, you have no business going to it. You have to bring it with you; you can't find it at the tournament."

Arrive prepared to win

The top shooters in any major tournament are extremely well prepared to be there. Although it may not look like it to a casual observer, the men and women who are shooting on the top targets are expertly organized and adequately rehearsed in all of their efforts to reach the top and stay there.

These people are prepared for almost any eventuality. They have consciously and subconsciously gone over the various potential situations in minute detail, figured out the best way to combat the problems, then prepared their equipment and themselves, both mentally and physically, to execute under pressure of important tournaments the chosen method of solving each potential problem.

This "preparing" has been done through practice, practice, practice under stress. It has all been done because top shooters understand fully that to achieve the results they want in this sport, they must leave nothing to chance.

There will always be enough unexpected things occurring on the day of a tournament to tend to change anyone's plans a little. The top performers, however, will have covered even these situations. They understand that there will be a solution to every problem and one that will work for them if they stay calm enough to think it through and then execute their plan.

Getting upset or uptight because one arrow didn't go into the group with the others will only help your competitor upgrade his confidence to a higher level, and then he'll gain by shooting better. You will already have lost a point or two on the arrow that didn't group. You can prevent any further losses by staying calm and re-establishing through intense concentration the fine control that you need to put the rest of your shots right where you expect them to go.

You know that after an arrow has hit the target, there is nothing you can do about it. For whatever reason it is out, it is out forever. That shot is now history, so you must accept it. No one says that you have to like it when you shoot out of your group, but you had better accept the fact that it is out, and it is out because of your lack of control somewhere in the execution of that shot.

You also know that no amount of feeling sorry for yourself will put that arrow back into the group where it belongs, but be sure you realize that if you continue to shoot with this attitude, you will experience a definite letdown in your efforts to correct a point or points of faulty control.

This must not be a popularly accepted fact, as you can see competitors oozing self-pity all over the shooting field at any tournament. It is 100 percent true. Comparative scores prove it. Accepting the shot and facing up to the reason for its being there is the mark of a true champion!

An important archer at an important tournament once made the statement that there were many people shooting who could actually shoot as well as he could, but that they didn't because they didn't know how.

That statement caused quite a stir among many who were present. They thought the remark was a put-down of all those people who were really trying hard on that particular day "to put it all together."

Many of the listeners interpreted this statement as an uncalled for and egotistical outburst on the part of the archer who was the high scorer at that point in the tournament.

It was an unfortunate interpretation and a complete misunderstanding of what this kind and humble man, this important archer and true champion, was trying to say. I had known this man for many years, and I knew that he was just stating an honest fact as he saw it. He felt there were other shooters whose form and shooting ability were comparable to his, but they did not know how to use this ability to their own best advantage. He felt they had never learned, as he had, that you not only had to be organized and well prepared prior to each shot, but that you need to maintain physical and mental control and concentration during the execution of the shot.

The point I'm trying to make here is practically the same thing, but I don't know that I can express it even as clearly as the archer did in the incident I just related. I do believe there is a degree of preparedness and consistent follow-through during competition of a champion's mind and body over and above what the average archer considers necessary.

I believe it is all-important for anyone who is in training to be organized and well prepared on all counts long before the day of competition. This most certainly includes learning to make honest and realistic judgments about what you can and cannot change. Through training, learn how to change the things that you can change and develop the ability to accept the things that you cannot change. Mind and body, concentration and control, is a double-barrelled attack weapon that can shoot down competition if you learn how to hold them until the shot is thoroughly completed.

> You learn to deal with losing long before you get to the Olympics, because you're sure not going to win all the time. Losing means nothing, and if you're too determined to win, any little disappointment will crush you.
>
> *Frank Shorter*

In my opinion, champion quality is made up of many little things which, in training, you do over and over again. If your heart is in the right place and if you can hold the right thoughts (attitudes) in your mind, the things which follow will work.

Simple little things like training yourself under any and all conditions to be able to concentrate until your arrow hits the target. Accept without reservation where the shot goes, but relax and put the next one where you want it to go. Practice developing a personal "cool cat" image. See that your competition thinks nothing bothers you. This will pay off.

What is the very best way to psych yourself up? The system which works for someone else might not be the best for you. Condition your mind by emphasizing the positive approach regarding all you intend to do at the upcoming tournament.

● *Arriving prepared to win means you will have, among other things, repeatedly shot under poor weather conditions so you know how you perform under less than ideal conditions.*

Consider losing to the competition. Accept a loss as just another brick in the pavement on the road to success. Set it in place smoothly and go on.

Consider different ways you can be a gracious winner. Practice humility and let what you have accomplished do the bragging for you. If you really deserve credit, the public will give it to you. If they don't, you'd better take a quick inventory, as you have undoubtedly missed an important cue somewhere.

Train yourself well to leave all the griping to someone else. It won't buy you anything you can use, and it will disrupt your positive thought flow.

Train yourself to sincerely welcome competition. Without it, you can never shoot your best. Practice with it every chance you get and learn from it.

Condition your body well with good exercise routines that will develop the kind of stamina you will most need. Eliminate all worry and doubt about your ability to shoot in wind, rain, cold, fog or whatever by repeatedly shooting under those conditions until you are confident that physical conditions like that will have no effect whatsoever upon your shooting.

It takes longer for some shooters than others to achieve a championship level of preparedness in all of these points. It may take weeks and weeks, or even years for some, but in every case, it is a reward well worth all the effort that went into it. I heartily recommend this kind of training.

I realize that if a burning desire and determination to shoot top target is not present, reading this may not be much help. However, I cannot stifle the hope that burns eternal that someone, somewhere, will catch a spark of desire and determination from these words that will eventually be fanned into the kind of flame that will produce a worthy competitor for all the other serious shooters around the world. **Prepare** yourself. You can be a champion!

It takes patience to be a good shooter.

Defining a "respectable" score

Years ago I learned to shut up and listen when a bunch of archers were talking about their shooting problems, their high and low points, their reasons for and against anything.

There is a vast amount of information that can be gleaned from these conversations if you will tune in, file them away and later dig them out, analyze them and then keep or discard them.

I believe this is important and advantageous to shooters as well as to coaches.

These conversations sometimes will point up the fact that we, too, are guilty of doing or thinking the same way that "he" does. We also know and have said that "he" is crazy as a loon for doing or thinking the way he does. The hard part for us is to wake up and admit that we also may be guilty of seeing something from the wrong angle.

Listening in on such a conversation during a recent tournament makes me want to talk to all the shooters who are trying to get their scores up to a **respectable level.** I am fully aware that this is a nebulous situation, as I hope to point out.

Several years ago, a young man came to me and asked for help in reaching a point where, in his words, he could shoot a respectable score. Not anything big or fancy, just a respectable score to take home and show his wife. He was a darned good shooter as he was, but I assured him that I thought we could improve his production of points for the score board without too much trouble.

I asked him what score he considered respectable. He said he had no specific number in mind. I asked if he could tell me **about** how high the score would have to be, to be respectable **for him.** He gave the state record.

I said, "I thought you just told me you didn't want to shoot anything big or fancy, just respectable."

"Yeah, that's right," he said.

● A "respectable" score is one that you yourself must judge on its merits as the situations and circumstances dictate at the time you are shooting. Judi Adams and Al Henderson are checking her score for the day at the National Archery Association of the United States national championship.

"Well, when I asked you to name a score that you could live with, you went all the way up to the state record."

"Yeah, what's wrong with that?"

I'm afraid I made a few remarks right about then that caused him to respond with, "Well, dammit, all I want is to go to a tournament just one time and shoot a score that doesn't make me look like a fool. Other people shoot respectable scores, and I am tired of being the one everyone knows is not doing so hot. I just want to shoot a score that's respectable, and I don't think it's crazy to want to do that."

I did not think him crazy, and I am happy to say that he got what he wanted but with different reasoning.

It seems to me that this true story points up several things that plague archers who want to shoot a respectable score but cannot ever do it to their satisfaction.

One reason is that they have no specific goal to strive for, no solid thing to hang onto, and, therefore, no way to tell when they get there. Another is that there is only one way to shoot a respectable score and that is to realize just where you are when you are trying to do it (meaning, what are your capabilities at that point in your archery career?) and then judge scores by these facts. We often kid ourselves by thinking one thing and doing another.

That is the same as saying, "I want the state record score, but I won't work for it. I will just keep it in limbo and hope for a respectable score, whatever that is."

I believe that in situations like this, we also are afraid we will get something we will be embarrassed to claim, because "they" will think it is not a respectable score.

Who are "they"? They're the people on target one, two, five, 16 or 20 who actually don't give a hoot whether your score is respectable or not. They don't share your concerns about your so-called problems.

You might think your score is not so hot, not up to par, not respectable. They may be more realistic and think, yes, that is about right for you, if they think of it at all.

What they think you have or have not achieved shouldn't bother you. The realistic yardstick is what you are capable of at the time the score is shot and how much honest effort you put into making it your best.

In my opinion, a **respectable** score is one that you yourself must judge on its merits as the situations and circumstances dictate at the time you are shooting. If you are fair to yourself, your equipment and your coach, you will consider all of the ramifications connected with your efforts and judge it for what it **really is,** not what you **wish** it was nor what you feel someone else **might think** it is.

There is only one person who can put the respectable label on a score you shoot. **You** are that person. It can be properly done only if you use the facts that are presented at that time and are honest to yourself and to those facts when you evaluate them. Seldom, if ever, would you come up with a score that you would not consider respectable, unless you just plain gave up and quit trying — in which case you get what you deserve. The lack of confidence in yourself, the frustrations and the wasting of the time and effort spent grinding out scores that are not, to you, respectable will be the price you will pay.

Consider what your goal really is and what you are willing to pay for it. If **you** and I don't include "he," "they" or "them," if you are strong enough, there is no handicap **fancied** or **real** big enough to keep you from reaching your goal — and **that** would be **respectable.**

Refuse to judge any of your work by what someone else thinks or does. Do your best constantly; therefore, what your efforts produce is respectable.

Failure to hit the bullseye is never the fault of the target.

Putting your form together

Every coach ought to be smart enough to learn from his or her students. Here's something I learned from Irene Daubenspeck.

We were at the Arizona state championship. She shot her six practice arrows and completely missed the target with one. She sure didn't seem loose to me, but then she stepped up there and shot two tens and a nine as her first three arrows for score.

I asked her later what was the matter with her on her practice arrows, and she said she didn't know. "What do you mean?" she asked.

"Well, you missed the target with one shot," I said, somewhat upset.

"Oh. I'm just putting my form together on the practice shots. I'm not trying to hit the gold."

That makes a lot of sense, and now I teach that. On your practice arrows, try to get the feel, how you're feeling that day. Stretch a little more, settle your mind in, get your confidence working and all that. You'll have that put together and out of the way before shooting for score begins. You don't care where the arrows go.

When the whistle blows, you've got everything ready to turn over to your subconscious to do the shooting. The partnership within you is working perfectly.

Half full?

When you go to a tournament, don't stand there and try to work out problems. You cannot try to be certain that this is working and that is working. Do that when you practice.

When you go to a tournament, shoot the tournament.

Never think "What's wrong?" when you should be thinking "How can I improve this?"

Is your glass half full or half empty? It depends upon how you look at it.

Handling ghosts, tournaments and other frights

What is there about a tournament that can take a perfectly sane, intelligent person in its grip and make that person act like a three-year-old kid afraid of the dark? What does it have that — after this person has practiced for weeks on end, is shooting super and knows he or she is ready for a win — can **and does** turn that sane, intelligent person into a shivering "fraidy cat" right in front of a hundred other shooters?

It may be that we should change the name of the event to something other than "tournament." How about switching things around? Since we always shoot super on the official practice ends and goof up when the tournament starts, how about giving us two official ends of tournament and then starting the practice ends for score?

It could be that the whistle causes all the trouble. I never had any trouble at tournaments until the field captain blew his whistle and said "This is it." Believe me, that's when Henderson got weak-kneed and stupid. I had a lot of long talks with him (Henderson) about this thing, and though he would admit how utterly ridiculous he was acting, he did not seem able to do anything to help it. Many, many years later I have discovered what the problem is and have proven to my satisfaction what is needed to fix it.

I believe that if we will, as a first step, try to understand that we and **we alone** cause the trouble and that we and **we alone** can fix it, then we can go on talking about it with some degree of success.

The hold that a tournament has on our good intentions is **fear** — fear exaggerated by our lack of self-control under the stress of a tournament. We become emotionally unstable, and that causes a breakdown in the physical part of our shooting. We have a fear of not performing as we want to or as we expect to. Or of what we **hope** we might do. If we go in with fear, we'll come out with disgust, for we're already second-guessing, alibiing, getting ready to not win. We are not scared of our opponent, we are scared of ourselves and what we **might** do or not do.

Learning to work at emotion control while on the shooting line is a must.

The best shooters of the world have the same problems all the time, but they are on top because they have **learned** how to **work** on control **while** they are in competition. They make it perform when they need it most. Too many shooters start out like tigers and finish like pussycats. The best shooters kick out the pussycat and make the tiger claw his way to the top.

I don't believe shooters know or realize they are not making any real attempt to control **emotions** at a tournament simply because they have never made any attempt to **learn how to gain control of themselves.**

As I observe shooters at any size tournament, I can definitely see when they give up or give in to the frustrations of tournament pressure. You can see the same thing in the other fellow. The advice to him is to cool it. But the other fellow can't cool it because he has never really learned how to work on the problem under tournament pressure.

How about you? Both of you have these problems, these frustrations, but only under tournament pressure, so at no time do you ever practice thinking about the problem and how you might improve the situation at the shoot.

All of us swear that we will lick it next time, but it will take more than that to fix it. However, we're so glad to get away from the frustrations of

● *Al Henderson and Judy Plants talk over a drawing elbow item and the general concerns which crop up during a tournament to cause control problems. To win, you must maintain control.*

the tournament that we almost run out the door to escape them. We have great intentions while we're still boiling, but those intentions are forgotten in a hurry.

It takes hard, mental work to set up those pressures in advance, to imagine them in practice. Few shooters do it.

In my opinion, you must know what the whole situation is and be realistic about everything involved. For instance, you cannot just read this, agree with it and then improve your tournament scores. **You must work at it.**

I believe you have to look eyeball to eyeball with yourself and learn to work when you don't want to. You must perfect your technique of self control so that at a tournament, big or small, you will have taught yourself the facts of life about what makes you shoot less than good when you try so hard. When you do understand that, you will understand what causes such erratic shooting. You will be able to work at teaching yourself the control, the cure.

Okay, so before an important tournament you faithfully practice every day, work out with weights, run three miles each morning. You are ready. Boy, are you ready!

Tournament Trail

Now you go to the tournament and do well the first day. You fell down some the morning of the second day, but did fine that afternoon and were on the board. Third day, you started out rotten and got worse as the day progressed. The fourth day, you did not start too hot, but you picked up and by afternoon were shooting your average or better.

But by then you had blown it, as you always do and knew you would. You don't understand it, really, because you worked so hard preparing. At the end, you hadn't even shot your average.

No one can say that you were not trying, were not sincere or in fact had done anything that you should not have done in preparing yourself for the shoot. You just had never understood that to keep all that other good work from being done for nothing, you must first learn to control your fears.

Think about this. **Everything** you do, no matter how insignificant, is controlled by your mind, as you command it. No way will you shoot any better until you understand and admit what your problem is, and then make the solving of that problem number one in your work.

You must concentrate on the performance of the form that you have worked so hard to perfect. Than at a tournament, under those intense pressures, you must put yourself into the same mental mood that you had when you were preparing for it and when you were shooting so well.

You must learn to replace those thoughts and emotions which cause you to tighten up (and blow the tournament) with a **positive** picture of how you can relax and stay that way. As you recapture the same mood and same feelings you had when you did your best shooting, concentrate on making them work now. You must make a great effort to continue with these moods, mental pictures and positive thoughts even when you seem to be shooting poorly. Concentrate hard, completely blocking out all things around you.

We blow tournaments because we hope to do something we are not emotionally prepared to do. We have never, fully worked at, and therefore have never fully learned, the commands which put our fear where it belongs — always present, but under control.

Most likely, the thing that scares you today is not knowing what is going to happen. I don't think you should wait and see what will happen. I think **you** should **control** what happens **today**.

Mark Twain said, "I have known a great many troubles, but most of them never happened."

Aid from the gallery

We're all human. We need the support of a gallery, be it one person or a dozen.

But that gallery also can set things awry without even trying.

I have a student whose father, when he is attending a tournament, can't help but keep asking her, "How'd you do that time? What was the matter? You did better the other time."

Now that is ridiculous. The girl knows her father. It is bound to upset her to some extent, and it does. She can't stop him. I can't stop him. He just is blind to what he's doing to her, when he thinks he's helping.

You must be careful if you are family, friend or whatever. I don't think you should ever ask a competitor how he or she is doing during a tournament. It is terribly wrong.

What you should say is, "To me, it looks good." Maybe you don't know anything about what's going on, and maybe you do. But that statement doesn't upset the shooter's applecart, it doesn't tell him anything that isn't true. The very fact that you said it, even though the archer knows he's not doing that well, makes him feel better having somebody tell him he looks good. That will help him relax, which will help his shooting.

The worst offense is when a member of the gallery, trying to be helpful, says to the shooter, "Someone standing back behind the line says you're dropping your bow arm." (The specific item could be any of a number of things, I just used bow arm here as an example.)

Someone else ought to smack that "friend" in the nose. He's doing nothing but tearing down.

When a shooter comes under stress, he often has a natural tendency to let a small flaw show itself. His guard is down because he's weakened a bit. Maybe the shooter was dropping his bow arm, but if he was shooting well, so what? The worst thing would be to focus attention on a known weakness of that student.

The coach has to keep the student's mind on positive things, not point out weaknesses. Encouragement of the right nature — work on the strengths — will do more to keep the shooter from lapsing back into that weakness.

In this case, the arrow was gone before the bow arm dropped, so what the "helpers" saw and what actually was happening were two different things. Only someone who is extremely familiar with your shooting would be able to pick up on the very small difference. You don't want to point out that a shooter is reverting back to old habits, because that gets the shooter negatively thinking right down the line.

The gallery can help you, and it can be the biggest stumbling block around. You want to share your good things, and you would like help to remain strong through the rough spots.

What is your real score?

Did you ever notice that at almost every tournament, large or small, you can generally hear one or more shooters complaining because they did not shoot a score they thought was good enough? It doesn't seem to matter what the score was, it just never was what they wanted or expected it to be.

Many times I have asked the shooter what kind of score he should have shot that would have satisfied his expectations. Every time, the answer was, "Well, better than this one."

Since that answer told me nothing, I'd press for a definite figure that would have pleased him or her. In every instance, the shooters could not give me an idea of what would be right. They just did not know.

If I asked what their average practice score was and got a specific figure, it would nearly always be within three or four points of the tournament score they had just shot.

I wonder what would make anyone think that under pressure of a tournament they could shoot much better scores than their practice.

Yes, anyone **can** shoot above their average in a tournament, and some do, but in my opinion the majority of shooters would be shooting better scores if they would be more realistic in their evaluations and expectations.

I knew a man who went to one of our most prestigious tournaments determined to shoot his average practice scores, and he won that championship. The interesting thing to me is that he shot one point above his average on both FITA rounds. It seems to me that a competitor would have a very negative attitude to cope with if he failed to look at this thing realistically.

If we have entered a tournament determined to do our best, and we shoot that tournament doing our best, then, where the shots go is a product of the best we could do at that tournament, under whatever conditions prevailed **that day.**

Now, if you did not do your best **that day,** I would hope that you would be the first to know it. If you couldn't prepare the shot so it felt good, couldn't seem to concentrate and your score was showing it, I would again hope that before you condemn yourself you will take into consideration a few facts that do concern every one of us.

In the first place, you are not a machine. The best you can do does not produce the same results every time. In spite of the fact that you are trying your best, things will go together on some days better than others. No way can you shoot the same score every tournament. No way can you **guarantee** that you will shoot the score you think you want.

There is nothing wrong with wanting to shoot a high score. There is nothing wrong in expecting to shoot a high score.

● *You can feel pride in yourself if you do your best each day at a tournament, regardless of your place in the tournament or the score you shot. You may or may not be satisfied with it, but you must accept it and carry on.*

It is wrong, though, if you did your **very best** on every shot, to give yourself the devil because you did not shoot the unrealistic score you wanted. The trick here, in the relationship with yourself, is to be realistic and **accept** whatever your score is, knowing full well that it was the best you could do that day. You don't have to like it, but you must **accept** it.

When you know that you did **not** do your best at that shoot, then I guess you have a right to complain about yourself. However, I am of the opinion that it will not help one bit. In fact, it is negative in nature and will erode some of the confidence you should have in yourself. Not many people can afford that.

I once had a student (national champion) who could not face me for days after she had shot a poor score. She always felt I would be ashamed of where she placed in the tournament.

I did not then, nor do I now, feel anything but pride for anyone who **does their best, that day,** regardless of their place in the tournament or for a score they might have shot.

Doing your best is a wonderful feeling, a prideful feeling, one that will give confidence to the worst of us. Doing our best should cancel out all negative feelings regarding the score. Again I say, if you do your best all through the tournament you may not be satisfied with it, but you must accept it. You shot it; it is gone; you can't shoot it over. Accept it with the confidence that on another day in another tournament it will be better because you know you are **doing your best.**

There is a problem that should be mentioned here. Great care must be exercised when we decide if **we are really** doing our best. It is a question we must be absolutely sure about. Even though we all think we are doing our best all the time, it isn't necessarily so. It is a sad situation when we kid ourselves into thinking we are trying our best, when in reality we are only coasting.

Many shooters claim they want to do it. These are the ones who have their words tangled up. They really are only wishing they could shoot better. It takes backbone, not wishbone, to succeed at anything. Always **doing our best,** not wishing, will pay off in more ways than just shooting arrows.

I believe it was O. J. Simpson who said, "Give it your best. If it doesn't work, it just wasn't your day that time."

Shoot in a tournament and work in practice. Don't work in a tournament and shoot in practice.

How did you shoot today?

All your friends and relatives are always trying to help you as a shooter, but often they ought just to leave you alone. Good intentions can cause a lot of trouble.

When someone asks "How did you shoot today?", the number one response is "Ah, I didn't do very well" or "A truck backfired and that threw me."

As a shooter, you have no business explaining anything to anyone at any time.

If someone asks me how I shot, I always say "I shot fine." Sometimes I say, "I shot fantastic." The person asking almost always doesn't care how I shot; that's just a social question. What he really wants to know is my score and whether or not he scored higher. So maybe you can just tell the person your score and keep on walking.

The next question invariably is "What happened?" That's no one else's business either. Maybe nothing wrong happened; you may have shot your best but didn't score all that well. A shooter must be a gentleman or a lady, but you can be that without getting into a negative situation. When you're asked "What went wrong?" you're automatically into a negative situation, unless you don't allow yourself to participate in the negative. You don't want to run yourself down. You want to prime yourself to shoot well tomorrow.

You can be the leading member of your cheering section.

I tell my students that, when they're on the line and feel a good shot, tell themselves that, give themselves a bit of congratulation, a positive boost. Even say it out loud if they want. You cannot disturb other people on the line, but you can talk to yourself.

(If a shooter can't handle the other people on the line, I'll help him. I simply say, "Oh, yeah, he talks to himself." There's nothing wrong with that. Besides, if the other shooter is hearing my student talk, he isn't concentrating the way he should be. He's letting negative influences into his shield of concentration . . . actually, he's letting outside neutral events become negative once they affect him.)

When you feel a good shot, say to yourself "Not bad, (first name)." When you shoot one that's a bit rough, say, "All right (name), let's clean it up a little bit." Get in that mood.

Ask any of the top people how they shot and they'll probably just tell you their score and stop there. They don't care whether you like how they shot, where they made their mistakes, or anything like that. You might comment that the wind was bad, but you also might not even get a response because the wind, as is the shooting, is done for the day. That's history.

You can also develop your own cheering section by recognizing the functions of your conscious mind and your subconscious. Your body is the subconscious named person and your mind is the conscious part. You (your mind) help you (your body) prepare the shot, and when you get that shot prepared you let your named body complete it. Your body carries through the explosion and follow through while your mind concentrates on where you believe the arrow will strike the target . . . where you want it . . . where you think it's going to go . . . where you believe it's going. That's all there is for your mind to do while your subconscious and your body carry out the memorized, grooved mechanics of the shot. Your subconscious knows how to shoot and will take care of its share of the work.

However, the split second your mind tries to help your subconscious and body put that arrow where you want it, you have messed up and the body won't shoot as well as it can.

This usually happens when you go to a tournament and begin to get a bit tight during shooting. You tighten up because you're trying to be careful, too careful. Your conscious begins trying to help your subconscious and body, but they already know how to shoot. They will do it perfectly if you will let them alone. Leave them alone and they probably will shoot arrows in the same hole, one right after another.

I believe this, and I have proved it time after time. It is so simple, yet so difficult to master.

The more you can assign the proper responsibilities to your

subconscious and your body, to the training they have in making the shot and feeling the shot, the better you will do. If you understand this principle, you'll come closer to doing it.

Your conscious can talk to your subconscious and your body, you can laugh at or with it, you can chide it, you can get mad at it — but not mad enough to throw a fit or get frustrated. Frustration won't help a bit, because your conscious mind is really controlling the remainder of you, except at the explosion of the shot.

You're loading the bow, drawing it, anchoring, getting your head position set, getting the string alignment, raising the sights and beginning to aim. It is at this moment, — when you begin to aim — that you let your subconscious and body take over. All your conscious does is aim. Aiming is concentration.

No one teaches you anything unless you learn it.

In baseball, a hitter who fails 70 percent of the time is acclaimed as among the best.

Chapter Seven: Coaches and Students

Your coach — the other half of a working pair

Five years or so ago at a gathering of archers, the subject of good shooting came up, as it most always does in such a group. And as is often the case, the conversation blossomed into a heated discussion on how you go about becoming a good shooter.

It was interesting and enlightening to listen in on this discussion. It was also interesting to note that 99 percent of the archers in the group agreed on the important things that get you to the top.

However, one individual disagreed on the idea that anyone needed a coach. This person was proud of the fact that he was 100 percent self-taught, had never asked anyone to coach him and wasn't going to because he didn't need one. He said he got where he was because he figured everything out for himself, applied it and made it work. What he didn't like, he discarded for something better.

Questions were thrown at him from several angles, one being why he changed from a high wrist on the bow to the low wrist that he was now using. His answer was that he checked and most good archers used the low wrist so he tried it and it worked.

The discussion got into just what is self-taught? What is meant when you say self-taught? Where does it start, where does it stop? In the end, he had to admit that perhaps some credit had to be given to the many people who answered his questions when he asked for information, and that if he were 100 percent self-taught he would have to have been a Robinson Crusoe on some lonely island teaching himself without help from any source.

After the discussion cooled down a bit, he still maintained he didn't need a coach. He flatly stated he wasn't that bad in the first place. He said he could not give anyone credit for his good shooting because he himself, not the coach, did the shooting. He felt that all the coach did was to straighten you out on something you could have straightened out yourself, and then the coach would want the credit when it was the shooter who won the tournament.

It was pointed out to him that the coach did not expect, nor did he ever

● In a working pair, the student supplies the desire, determination, understanding, concentration, practice and performance. The coach reinforces, encourages, regulates and programs the student and helps supply the technology. They put it all together — together.

receive, any credit for the student's physical endeavors as such, but that the coach deserved the honor and the satisfaction of having a student who could **understand** and respond to a team effort, and who was intelligent and determined enough to play the game and win.

It was also pointed out to him that any coach or student who faces facts (and the good ones do) knows that the coach does not put the physical form together, hold the bow, pull the string, anchor the hand, keep the tension, aim the pins, or give the command that triggers the explosion of the shot. Neither does the coach expect or get credit for those physical acts by the student.

The physical structure of the student's form must be learned, assembled and executed by the student. The student's physical form is the combination of the student's abilities and the coach's efforts. The coach's skill in instilling into his student's mental process what it takes to command and control the complexities of a good shot — and the student's **understanding** and acceptance of these things — are what produces a winning team.

That is what the coach takes pride in and accepts credit for.

It is no crime to ask for and accept help from another source. Name a top golfer who didn't use a coach to learn the game properly when he started and who refuses to use one to keep his game in top shape. I don't think you can.

Ask any swimmer, tennis player, skater or diver if he or she thinks a coach is necessary to prepare for the stiff competition of today.

The student supplies the desire, determination, understanding, concentration, practice and performance on the line.

The coach reinforces, encourages, regulates and programs the student and helps supply the technology.

They put it all together — together.

What a joy for the student when he proudly walks into the winner's circle; what a thrill for the coach standing on the outside; what a satisfaction to them both for a team effort well done.

The right type of coach and student communication

A shooter-student can do a lot to help his coach, and in so doing he (the shooter) will benefit more and quicker. If you want the most from your coach, you will talk freely, very freely, to your coach about your beliefs. You don't need to get embarrassingly personal, but the better the coach understands how you tick, the better he'll be able to help you.

If the coach says, "You look like this," you could say, "But I sure don't feel like that."

I would be elated at a response like that, because it would say that one of us has to get on the ball. So I'd ask, "How **did** it feel?"

The student might stumble around a little trying to put it into words, and I might stumble around a little, too. But we'd work on it together, and we'd figure it out.

The student needs to talk about his archery thoughts and what he's doing . . . especially about his thoughts . . . how he feels, his frustrations. He has to contribute the difficult part — he has to talk about himself.

He also has to ask questions. If something isn't clear, ask. That's the only way you will fully understand.

The student can't observe himself like the coach can observe him because he's not objective and has mental blocks. The coach may not be as objective as he should be and may also have some mental blocks, but they shouldn't be as personal (toward the student) or as large as the student's. The coach can't provide the background that the student can. The two together can fill in the blanks, work that crossword puzzle until you get the answers.

If I had my d'ruthers

The editor of this book asked me once, "What would be the ideal circumstance for a coach and a shooter?"

The answer: That they understand each other 100 percent and can communicate 100 percent. Man, you could go like a house afire.

As a coach, my goal is to make you understand the various aspects of winning archery. That will go a long way toward helping you become a winning archer. You can have the drive and the desire and do all the necessary practice, but if you don't truly understand it, it won't work. The explanations may get lengthy, but they're necessary.

How else could you, the shooter, stand on the shooting line and be best prepared? You have to know why you did or did not do certain things, and you have to understand the reasons for them. Without that, you don't have the bedrock to fall back on when things don't work quite as you wanted them to work. If someone said, "Eat blue pine needles on Sunday. It will make you a winner," well what happens when you get to a tournament and no restaurant is serving blue pine needles? You have to have the foundation to provide some of your own insight and keep your strengths flowing. You have to be able to relate to something, and you have to be flexible enough in your confidence to handle something that might be a little bit unexpected. You cannot anticipate everything, nor should you try. You may have to do things you don't really want to do.

You are alone on the shooting line. If you put your shot together right, have confidence, believe, and then do your best that day, we'll all be proud of you no matter what the score. And you should be proud of yourself.

COOPERATION PAYS